THE SNOW WALKER
by
Farley Mowat

"Excellent . . . These are stories that have a deep emotional content; they are spiritually moving in the way that good fiction should be . . ."

—Books in Canada

"Powerful and unusual. The Snow Walker is a book about a harsh environment and about human beings extended into that rare realm of heroism. The tales are told in a style that is both entertaining and illuminating."

—Boston Herald Advertiser

"Farley Mowat re-establishes himself as that figure honored in both primitive and advanced communities, the master storyteller. His tales are compelling, though the unifying thread running through them traces a grisly line . . . Mowat is superb at creating mood, personalities and relationships."

—San Francisco Examiner-Chronicle

THE SNOW WALKER

Farley Mowat

SEAL BOOKS
McClelland and Stewart-Bantam Limited
Toronto

*This low-priced Seal Book
has been completely reset in a type face
designed for easy reading, and was printed
from new plates. It contains the complete
text of the original hard-cover edition.*
NOT ONE WORD HAS BEEN OMITTED.

THE SNOW WALKER

*A Seal Book / published by arrangement with
McClelland and Stewart Limited*

PRINTING HISTORY

McClelland and Stewart edition published June 1975
2nd printing ... October 1975   3rd printing .. November 1975
4th printing ... January 1976
Seal edition / November 1977
2nd printing . November 1977   5th printing ..... July 1980
3rd printing .. February 1978   6th printing .. December 1981
4th printing .... April 1979   7th printing .. November 1983
8th printing ... December 1984

ISBN 0-7704-2058-3

PRINTED IN THE UNITED STATES OF AMERICA

H   17 16 15 14 13 12 11 10

Contents

Snow 1

The Blinding of André Maloche 11

Stranger in Taransay 35

The Iron Men 51

Two Who Were One 68

The Blood in Their Veins 84

The Woman and the Wolf 104

The Snow Walker 120

Walk Well, My Brother 132

The White Canoe 149

Dark Odyssey of of Soosie 172

*Where there is merit in this book
it is in no small part due to the unremitting,
gentle but implacable persistence of Lily Miller.
Where the work falters it is because
sometimes I neglected to listen to her.*

THE SNOW WALKER

Snow

When Man was still very young he had already become aware that certain elemental forces dominated
the world womb. Embedded on the shores of their
warm sea, the Greeks defined these as Fire and Earth
and Air and Water. But at first the Greek sphere was
small and circumscribed and the Greeks did not recognize the fifth elemental.

About 330 B.C., a peripatetic Greek mathemati-
cian named Pytheas made a fantastic voyage northward to Iceland and on into the Greenland Sea. Here
he encountered the fifth elemental in all of its white
and frigid majesty, and when he returned to the warm
blue Mediterranean, he described what he had seen
as best he could. His fellow countrymen concluded
he must be a liar since even their vivid imaginations
could not conceive of the splendour and power in-
herent in the white substance that sometimes lightly

cloaked the mountain homes of their high-dwelling Gods.

Their failure to recognize the immense power of snow was not entirely their fault. We who are the Greeks' inheritors have much the same trouble comprehending its essential magnitude.

How do *we* envisage snow?

It is the fragility of Christmas dreams sintering through azure darkness to the accompaniment of the sound of sleigh bells.

It is the bleak reality of a stalled car and spinning wheels impinging on the neat time schedule of our self-importance.

It is the invitation that glows ephemeral on a woman's lashes on a winter night.

It is the resignation of suburban housewives as they skin wet snowsuits from runny-nosed progeny.

It is the sweet gloss of memory in the failing eyes of the old as they recall the white days of childhood.

It is the banality of a TV advertisement pimping Coca Cola on a snowbank at Sun Valley.

It is the gentility of utter silence in the muffled heart of a snow-clad forest.

It is the brittle wind-rush of skis; and the bellicose chatter of snowmobiles.

Snow is these things to us, together with many related images; yet all deal only with obvious aspects of a multifaceted, kaleidoscopic and protean element.

Snow, which on our planet is a phoenix continually born again from its own dissolution, is also a galactic and immortal presence. In the nullity of outer space, clouds of snow crystals, immeasurably vast, drift with time, unchanged since long before our world was born, unchangeable when it will be gone.

2

For all that the best brains of science and the sharpest of the cyclopean eyes of astronomers can tell, the glittering crystals flecking the illimitable void are as one with those that settle on our hands and faces out of the still skies of a December night.

Snow is a single flake caught for an instant on a windowpane. But it is also a signboard in the solar system. When astronomers peer up at Mars they see the Red Planet as a monochromatic globe—except for its polar caps from which gleaming mantles spread toward the equatorial regions. As the antelope flashes its white rump on the dun prairies, so does Mars signal to worlds beyond it with the brilliance of our common sun reflected from its plains of snow.

And so does Earth.

When the first star voyager arcs into deep space, he will watch the greens and blues of our seas and lands dissolve and fade as the globe diminishes until the last thing to beacon the disappearing Earth will be the glare of our own polar heliographs. Snow will be the last of the elementals in his distant eye. Snow may provide the first shining glimpse of our world to inbound aliens ... if they have eyes with which to see.

Snow is crystalline dust, tenuous amongst the stars; but on Earth it is, in yet another guise, the Master Titan. To the south it holds the entire continent of Antarctica in absolute thrall. To the north it crouches heavily upon mountain ranges; and the island subcontinent of Greenland literally sags and sinks beneath its weight. For glaciers are but another guise of snow.

Glaciers are born while the snow falls; fragile, soft and almost disembodied ... but falling steadily without a thawing time. Years pass, decades, centuries, and the snow falls. Now there is weight where there

3

was none. At the surface of an undulating white waste, there seems to be no alteration, but in the frigid depths the crystals are deformed; they change in structure, interlock with increasing intimacy and eventually meld into black, lightless ice.

Four times during Earth's most recent geological age snow fell like this across much of the northern half of our continent and in Europe and Asia too. Each time, snow altered the face of almost half a world. A creeping glacial nemesis as much as two miles thick oozed outward from vast central domes, excoriating the planet's face, stripping it of life and soil, ripping deep wounds into the primordial rock and literally depressing Earth's stone mantle hundreds of feet below its former level. The snow fell, softly, steadily, until countless millions of tons of water had vanished from the seas, locked up within the glaciers; and the seas themselves withdrew from the edges of the continents.

There is no natural phenomenon known to us that can surpass the dispassionate power of a great glacier. The rupturing of Earth during its most appalling earthquake cannot compare with it. The raging water of the seas in their most violent moments cannot begin to match it. Air, howling in the dementia of hurricanes, is nothing beside it. The inner fire that blows a mountain to pieces and inundates the surrounding plains with floods of flaming lava is weak by comparison.

A glacier is the macrocosmic form of snow. But in its microscopic forms, snow epitomizes ethereal beauty. It is a cliché to say that no two snowflakes are identical, but it is a fact that each single snowflake that has fallen throughout all of time, and that will fall through what remains of time, has been—will be—a unique creation in symmetry and form.

I know of one man who has devoted most of his adult life to the study of this transient miracle. He has built a special house fitted with a freezing system, instead of heating equipment. It is a house with a gaping hole in its roof. On snowy days and nights he sits in icy solitude catching the falling flakes on plates of pre-chilled glass and hurriedly photographing them through an enlarging lens. For him the fifth elemental in its infinite diversity and singularity is beauty incarnate, and a thing to worship.

Few of us would be of a mind to share his almost medieval passion. In truth, modern man has insensibly begun to develop a schizophrenic attitude toward the fifth elemental. Although we may remember our childhood experience of it with nostalgia, more and more we have begun to think of snow with enmity. We cannot control snow, nor bend it to our will. The snow that fell harmlessly and beneficently upon the natural world our forefathers lived in has the power to inflict chaos on the mechanical new world we have been building. A heavy snowfall in New York, Montreal, Chicago, produces a paralytic stroke. Beyond the congealed cities it chokes the arteries of our highways, blocks trains, grounds aircraft, fells power and telephone cables. Even a moderate snowfall causes heavy inconvenience—if smashed cars, broken bodies, and customers for the undertakers are only inconveniences.

We will probably come to like snow even less. Stories about the good old-fashioned winters when snow mounted to the eaves of houses and horse-hauled sleighs were galloped over drifts at tree-top level are not just old wives' tales. A hundred years ago such happenings were commonplace. However, during the past century our climate has experienced a warming trend, an upswing (from our point of view), in the erratic cyclic variations of the weather. It has probably been a short-term swing and the downswing may soon be upon us. And where will we be then, poor things, in our delicately structured artificial world? Will we still admire snow? More likely we will curse the very word.

However, when that time comes there may still be men alive who will be unperturbed by the gentle, implacable downward drift. They are the true people of the snows.

They live only in the northern hemisphere because the realm of snow in the southern hemisphere —Antarctica—will not permit the existence of any human life unless equipped with a panoply of protective devices not far short of what a spaceman needs. The snow people ring the North Pole. They are the Aleuts, Eskimos and Athapascan Indians of North America; the Greenlanders; the Lapps, Nensi, Chukchee, Yakuts, Yukagirs and related peoples of Eurasia and Siberia.

Cocooned in the machine age, we smugly assume that because these people live unarmoured by our ornate technology, they must lead the most marginal kind of existence, faced with so fierce a battle to survive that they have no chance to realize the "human potential." Hard as it may strike into our dogmatic belief that technology offers the only valid way of life, I can testify from my own experiences with many of the snow people that this assumption is wrong. They mostly lived good lives, before our greed and our megalomaniac arrogance impelled us to meddle in their affairs. That is, if it be good to live at peace with oneself and one's fellowmen, to be in harmony with one's environment, to laugh and love without restraint, to know fulfilment in one's daily life, and to rest from birth to death upon a sure and certain pride.

6

Snow was these people's ally. It was their protection and their shelter from abysmal cold. Eskimos built complete houses of snow blocks. When heated only with simple animal-oil lamps, these had comfortable interior temperatures, while outside the wind screamed unheard and the mercury dropped to fifty degrees or more below zero. Compacted snow provides nearly perfect insulation. It can be cut and shaped much more easily than wood. It is light to handle and strong, if properly used. A snowhouse with an inner diameter of twenty feet and a height of ten feet can be built by two men in two hours. On special occasions Eskimos used to build snowhouses fifty feet in diameter and, by linking several such together, formed veritable snow mansions.

All of the snow people use snow for shelter in one way or another. If they are sedentary folk possessing wooden houses, they bank their homes with thick snow walls in wintertime. Some dig a basement in a snowdrift and roof it with reindeer skins. As long as snow is plentiful, the peoples of the far north seldom suffer serious discomfort from the cold.

Snow also makes possible their transportation system. With dog sleds and reindeer sleds, or afoot on snowshoes or trail skis, they can travel almost anywhere. The whole of the snow world becomes a highway. They can travel at speed, too. A dog or reindeer team can move at twenty miles an hour and easily cover a hundred miles a day.

The mobility snow gives them, combined with the way snow modifies the behavior of game animals, ensures that—other things being equal—the snow people need not go hungry. Out on the arctic ice a covering of snow gives the seals a sense of false security. They make breathing holes in the ice, roofed by a thin layer of snow. The Chukchee or Eskimo hunter

7

finds these places and waits beside them until, at a signal from a tell-tale wand of ivory or wood inserted in the roof, he plunges his spear down into the unseen animal below.

In wooded country, moose, elk and deer are forced by deep snow to "yard" in constricted areas where they can be killed nearly as easily as cattle in a pen. Most important of all, every animal, save those with wings and those who live beneath the snow, leaves tracks upon its surface. From bears to hares they become more vulnerable to the human hunter as soon as the first snow coats the land.

The snow people know snow as they know themselves. In these days our scientists are busy studying the fifth elemental, not so much out of scientific curiosity but because we are anxious to hasten the rape of the north or fear we may have to fight wars in the lands of snow. With vast expenditures of time and money, the scientists have begun to separate the innumerable varieties of snow and to give them names. They could have saved themselves the trouble. Eskimos have more than a hundred compound words to express different varieties and conditions of snow. The Lapps have almost as many. Yukagir reindeer herdsmen on the arctic coast of Siberia can tell the depth of snow cover, its degree of compactness, and the amount of internal ice crystallization it contains simply by glancing at the surface.

The northern people are happy when snow lies heavy on the land. They welcome the first snow in autumn, and often regret its passing in the spring. Snow is their friend. Without it they would have perished or—almost worse from their point of view—they would long since have been driven south to join us in our frenetic rush to wherever it is that we are bound.

8

Somewhere, on this day, the snow is falling. It may be sifting thinly on the cold sands of a desert, spreading a strange pallidity and flecking the dark, upturned faces of a band of Semitic nomads. For them it is in the nature of a miracle; and it is certainly an omen and they are filled with awe and chilled with apprehension.

It may be whirling fiercely over the naked sweep of frozen plain in the Siberian steppe, or on the Canadian prairies, obliterating summer landmarks, climbing in scimitar drifts to wall up doors and windows of farmhouses. Inside, the people wait in patience. While the blizzard blows, they rest; when it is over, work will begin again. And in the spring the melted snows will water the new growth springing out of the black earth.

It may be settling in great flakes on a calm night over a vast city; spinning cones of distorted vision in the headlights of creeping cars and covering the wounds, softening the suppurating ugliness inflicted on the earth by modern man. Children hope it will continue all night long so that no buses, street cars or family automobiles will be able to carry the victims off to school in the morning. But adult men and women wait impatiently, for if it does not stop soon the snow will smother the intricate designs that have been ordained for the next day's pattern of existence.

Or the snow may be slanting swiftly down across a cluster of tents huddled below a rock ridge on the arctic tundra. Gradually it enfolds a pack of dogs who lie, noses thrust under bushy tails, until the snow covers them completely and they sleep warm. Inside the tents men and women smile. Tomorrow the snow may be deep enough and hard enough so that the tents can be abandoned and the welcome domes of snow-houses can rise again to turn winter into a time of gaiety, of songs, of leisure and lovemaking.

Somewhere the snow is falling.

The Blinding of André Maloche

When I arrived at Caribou there were only two other white men in the settlement: Father Jean-Guy Danioux and his lay brother, André Maloche. The rest of the human population consisted of a dozen Cree families, ten or twelve half-breeds and about ninety Chipewyans; although the Chips could hardly be considered residents since we only saw them three or four times a year when they drifted in to trade or to attend one of the religious festivals.

My posting to Caribou had come about by accident. I'd been spending the last few days of my annual leave from my own post (it was in the western arctic), visiting friends in Winnipeg, when the Caribou post manager had a heart attack and had to be flown out. The Company's fur-trade commissioner tracked me down and asked me to fill in until he could find a permanent replacement. Because Caribou had the reputation of being about the most isolated and old-fashioned trading post in the Company's domains, I was curious to see it, so I agreed.

There was no doubt about the isolation. It lay six hundred miles north of Winnipeg, a good way north even of the old trade canoe routes. Freight reached it only once a year by tractor train from The Pas, which was the nearest real settlement. The cat train usually took five weeks to make the round trip over frozen muskegs, across the ice of dozens of rivers and lakes, through the thinning forests of black spruce and jack pine.

I went in by air in an old Fairchild float plane of the stick-and-string variety flown by a pilot whose main claim to fame was that he had written off seven airplanes and had managed to walk away more or less uninjured from each of them.

The settlement itself consisted of a score of scrofulous log shanties flung any-old-which-way across a desolate sand ridge on the north shore of Caribou Lake. Right in the middle was a hog-backed log church with a corrugated iron roof. At the north end of the ridge stood the cluster of red-and-white-painted Company buildings, the store, a little warehouse and the manager's cabin.

Stories about Caribou were legion throughout the north. Most of them grew up around the iron-bound nature of the man who was as good as King of a district as big as Scotland—Father Danioux, a whipcord bundle of ancient sinews, with a long white beard and a piece of trap steel for a backbone. When the Father came to Caribou from France half a century earlier, he immediately set about building a kind of church-state. He took hold of the Indians, both Chips and Crees, and punched and twisted and bent them into the shape he had in mind. Though some of them tried, they couldn't stand up against him because he could beat them even at their own game. Anything an Indian could do, Danioux learned to do better. It wasn't long before he was the absolute boss of a little theocracy that functioned like something out of the Old Testament. If one of the Indians backslid, Danioux thought nothing of taking a dogwhip to him. One of the stories about him had to do with the trouble he ran into with an old Chip medicine man who tried to buck him in the early days. Danioux solved that problem during an epic confrontation by putting a bullet through the man's skull.

Father Danioux hated outsiders—not that many such ever found their way to the Caribou country. If they did, they got nowhere with the natives because Danioux forbade "his people" to have anything to do with other white men. He barely tolerated the Company post because he needed us to bring in supplies; but he took a good fat tithe of furs from the Indians *before* they were allowed to trade for the flour, guns, tea, ammunition and the few other things he allowed them to buy.

The commissioner had taken pains to brief me about him:

"Treat him with kid gloves. Don't ever cross him. The old bugger runs the show at Caribou!"

Danioux's relations with me were as icy as the arctic winds that cut through the thin trees from the barrenlands not far to the north of us. He ordered the natives to have no more to do with me than was absolutely necessary, and he never deigned to come near the post himself. When he had a message for me —more like an imperial edict—Brother Maloche would bring it over, feeling his way through the rabble of half-starved dogs with great agility, considering that he was stone blind.

I had had enough of the place before the first

month was out, and I started banging out radio messages to head office in Winnipeg reminding the commissioner I was only filling in and asking when the permanent replacement would arrive. When I received only evasive answers, I began to realize that finding anybody else to take on the job looked like a long-term problem. Finally I resigned myself to spending the winter there. I wasn't entirely unhappy about the prospect thanks to a mass of books left behind by my predecessor . . . and to the friendship of André Maloche.

André and I took to each other right from the start. The non-fraternizing edict did not seem to apply to him and he would visit me two or three times a week. We would sit close to the angry glow of my sheet-iron stove trading stories about the north or just yarning. He was a big man, and gaunt. Under his thick, white eyebrows the empty eye sockets were impenetrable black pits that discouraged me from probing too deeply into what lay behind them. He was a private man, but a friend worth having. His serenity and his quiet sense of humour were marvellous antidotes against the loneliness of the long winter nights.

My affection for him grew in direct proportion to my dislike of the priest. The everyday details of men's lives in such an isolated little world as ours had to be common knowledge and so I came to know a good deal about how Danioux treated his lay brother. For nearly half a century André had lived under the biting goad of an austere and iron-willed autocrat whose religious ideas bordered on the fanatical. Through those long decades Danioux had used André as a sort of spiritual whipping boy while physically treating him like a serf. The wonder of it was that André, who was no weakling either physically or mentally, should have accepted it. One night I overstepped myself and made an oblique display of my indignation.

"My friend," André replied gently. "Do not think too harshly of *le bon Père*. At heart he is a saintly man. His life has been a hard struggle against heathen unbelief. Moreover, he has much to bear; and if at times he grows impatient with the load he carries, that is excusable."

I grunted sceptically.

"Perhaps you will understand," he continued, "if I tell you that my treatment at his hands is just. It is deserved. Because, you see, *I* am a cross he has to bear."

I did not understand but André volunteered no further explanation. We chatted idly until it was time for him to return to the frigid little room which was his home in the log shanty that served as a mission residence.

A few days later my half-breed clerk told me Father Danioux was seriously ill. I sent over to the mission to see if I could be of any help but, over the years, André had become an effective if rough and ready man with a scalpel or a pill. He was already dosing Danioux with sulfa, and did not need me to confirm his diagnosis. It was pneumonia—the Old Man's Friend, as my grandfather used to call it.

When the time came for my regular radio schedule that night, I tapped out a message asking for an emergency flight. A Norseman started out from The Pas next day but ran into bad weather and had to turn back. For a week after that we had nothing but storms, and not even the white owls could move. André stayed by the bed of the sick man night and day, nursing him with the dedication of a wife . . . but one afternoon the bell of the little church began

15

to toll. Danioux was dead. They put his rough coffin on a trellis of spruce poles high above the frozen earth which could not receive him until the ground thawed in spring.

It was some time before André came to visit me again, and when he did there was a great change in him. He had become even more gaunt—almost skeletal—but his face had lost its masked, impervious look. The years seemed to have fallen away from him. I thought this was a reflection of his relief at coming to the end of fifty years of wearing Danioux's saddle. It was more than that.

We drank coffee for awhile, then André spoke softly as if to himself.

"Finished. *C'est fini.*"

He turned his blind face toward me.

"Maybe you will be patient with an old man if he opens up his heart? It has been closed too long. Always I have lived alone with this thing. You would do me much kindness if you would listen."

Then he told me a story so strange that to this day I cannot be sure if it was real or even what it means.

You know I came from a little farm near Dauphin, eh? Lots of children in my family. But my father, he was killed in the bush, cutting pulp, when I was nine, and after that it was not long before my mother died. The Church took pity on us children. Me, I went first to an orphanage but when I was older I was sent to the seminary. They wished to make a priest of me, but that could not be. No, I was too wild for that. For me there was just the woods and the rivers and, best of all, the life my mother's people lived, for they were of the Salteaux. So one day I ran away and went to live with the Salteaux. But the priest they had there

16

soon found out about me and I was taken back. Then I was very angry and foolish. I made so much trouble they would lock me up in a room for days. I got more angry, and one night I took matches and a candle and started a fire in the dormitory and then I ran away again.

This time I was not caught, for I went too far; up to The Pas, and then with an old trapper to Athabasca Lake. He died when I was eighteen and I took over his outfit and went trapping on my own. I was twenty when I first came to the Caribou Lake country, and that winter I trapped mink and muskrats up toward Wollaston.

One time I was visiting a Chipewyan camp and old Denikazi—in those days he was the chief and a great traveller—told me about the *Esquimaux* who lived up to the north in the tundra. Denikazi had met some of them at tree line when they came south to get wood. He had played *udzi* with them, gambling for dogs. His stories gave me a hunger to visit those lands of mystery where it was said the muskox still lived and the so-beautiful white foxes could be found in such numbers a man could make a fortune in a single season.

Denikazi said the best time to travel in the tundra plains was late in the winter. So in February I drove to Caribou and traded my furs for ammunition, tea, lard, flour and bacon. I was here in your store, talking to the manager, when the young priest in charge of the mission came in. Father Danioux was only a few years older than me. He was on fire with the idea to bring all the Indians to God, but he had also heard of the Esquimaux no white men had ever visited, and he had heard I was going to try and reach their country.

He wanted me to take him with me so he could claim them for God also, but I did not like priests.

I did not even go to mass anymore. When I refused, the Father became angry and threatened he would drive me out of the Faith altogether if I would not help in God's holy work. That bothered me, to tell the truth, but I did not let him see. I said he could do what he wanted, but me, I was travelling alone.

So off I went to the north . . . and what a fine journey that was! Inside the forests there was plenty of deer so when I got to the edge of their winter yards I made a camp, killed lots of caribou, and dried the meat over smoky fires. When I had as much meat as my nine dogs could haul, I drove on again. My dogs and me, we were all strong and young, and we felt good. We travelled fast and hard and we were happy —I was going into a land nobody else had visited, and my dogs had full bellies and maybe they felt the same excitement.

The trees grew thinner and shorter along the shores of frozen rivers until there were no more trees at all. There was only a white plain, rolling farther than I could see from the top of the highest hills. I thought: How will I find the Esquimos in so big a country? I did not know how but I was sure to try.

Big rivers still pointed north so I drove on their ice. Sometimes I would find a clump of willows in the lee of a hill and then I would have a little fire; but for the most part there was nothing to burn, so the dogs and I ate our meat frozen and dry, but it was good, strong stuff and we did not mind. When the winds blew hard we could not travel. The north wind cut through my fur *capote* like it was made of fish net, and the ground drift would get so thick I could not even see my lead dog—but most of the time there was little wind and the sky was so big and cold and clear it was like there was no top over that land at all.

Every day I was sure I would find some sign of the Esquimos but always those big white plains stayed empty except for a few hares and white owls and the tracks of a wolf or a fox. There was no sign of men. Then, eight or nine days after I left the forests behind me, I saw a big ridge on the horizon. When I got closer I saw three figures on top of it and they looked like men. I was a little scared but I drove on, and the figures never moved, and that made me feel more uneasy. Before I started up the slope I slipped my rifle out of its case, but when I got to the top I found those figures were just made of piled-up stones.

It was a disappointment, you understand, but not too bad because those figures had been *made* by men, for sure. And when I drove on over that ridge I went down into a deep valley and found a real oasis. It was a stand of black spruce, maybe fifty acres. The trees were small, but they were *real* trees! My team went tearing in among them and I put my arms around one of the dwarf trunks and gave it a big hug. I looked around. Somebody else had found that place before me. Here and there were stumps where someone had been cutting timber, but they were all old cuttings.

I hadn't found the Esquimos, but now it was time for me to settle down to make a camp. That same day I began chopping logs for a cabin. Those trees were frozen solid right to the middle and my axe would jump back out of the cuts like it was crazy. All the same, in three days I had the walls of a cabin eight feet by eight. I roofed it with poles, then caribou skins, then blocks of hard snow. When I put my little tin stove inside, it was snug but there was no room in there to have a dance!

For the next few weeks things went well and I was happy. There was plenty of fox tracks and I set out a big bunch of traps. I had not much meat to spare for bait, but that did not matter. Those foxes were so tame they were pushing each other away to get caught. That was fine for awhile, but then I began to see this was really a hungry land. I drove my dogs hundreds of miles around that place and never found game. My store of meat began to run out. I tried to set a net under the river ice, but that ice was ten feet thick . . . impossible! Soon I had to feed the dogs with fox carcasses, and then I had to eat fox myself. I began to wonder if I was foolish to come out into this country. The cold was terrible and it kept me busy cutting wood for my stove, and just as busy making it burn for it was all green stuff.

I began to lose heart a little. The emptiness of that country was worse than the cold. Once I saw a raven and I thought it might mean a little herd of deer starting north out of the forest but when I drove south for nearly a day I never saw a living thing. The foxes vanished. Maybe I'd caught them all, but anyway the traps were empty. Late in March things got serious. I could not feed all my dogs anymore. I had to kill some to feed the others.

Denikazi had told me the caribou would start north in April or early May, and so it would be all right if I could hang on until the deer herds reached my place. There was only one way to do that. I killed the rest of my dogs and began to eat them myself. They were not much good for me. They were starved and the meat was bitter and there was no fat, but they kept me alive anyway.

Yes, I kept alive, but by the end of April the deer had not come and I was very weak and also sick from eating starving dog meat. I thought: well, that's the end of it. I was pretty near gone when one day I heard dogs yelping, and a man's voice.

They say you don't believe what you hear when you are pretty near dead . . . but *I* believed it! I crawled out of my bunk and got the skin door pulled open and nearly fell outside. There, right in front of my cabin, was a long wooden sled and three little men staring up toward me. Esquimos, for sure! I started toward them, staggering like a drunken fool, and they caught me when I fell.

You will perhaps not believe what those *sauvages* did next. Remember, they had never seen a white man in all their lives. The only strangers they knew about were the Chipewyans and, except for a few like Denikazi, the Chips hated the Esquimos and would shoot them when they got a chance.

What did they do? They carried me to my cabin and put me in my robes and piled their own robes on me. Then they cleaned out the place—it was worse than a bear's den—and for three days they nursed me, day and night, with meat soups and marrow and all sorts of stuff I never heard of. While I began to get some strength, they talked away to me in their own language and laughed and grinned and sang songs, and they brought my spirit back to life the same as they brought my body back.

In three days I was feeling good again. They wanted me to go with them, so we cached my cariole and some of my gear and I rode off on their long sled to their camps, four days' travel northwest. They had six snowhouses under the lee of a big hill by the shores of a frozen lake, and thirty-five people lived in that place.

Those Esquimos—*Innuit*, they called themselves —they were the fine people. Everything they had they gave to me, and I could give them nothing but endless trouble. They taught me their language, with a patience we do not often have even for our own

21

children. They gave me affection and friendship as wholehearted as it was tolerant. And ... they gave me my wife, a girl of my own choosing.

Her name was Nuljalik, the daughter of Katelo, one of those men who found me at my cabin. I think she was no more than seventeen years old; a small person, slim and almond eyed, and a round red face like a good, sweet apple. She had a slow smile that warmed me better even than the good food Katelo's old wife made for me. Katelo was quick to see the looks that passed between his daughter and me. One night when we were all climbing under the robes in his big deerskin tent, he said to me, simply, because I did not yet know so many Innuit words:

"*Schweenack*—not good for man to sleep alone. Here is *arnuk*, a woman for you. Take her, Saluk (that was the name they had given me). She is willing."

Nuljalik came to me in the new tent those people built for us, and the love she gave me was of a kind our race, perhaps, has forgotten. She kept nothing of herself away from me and expected me to do the same. That was a hard lesson for me to learn, how to give without holding back, but Nuljalik showed me the way.

It had been in my mind that when the summer came I would try to walk south out of the plains country; but as time went along and the birds and caribou and flowers filled the long days with sights and sounds and smells, I told myself it was foolish to try to walk south. I would wait, and in the winter Katelo would take me south with his dog team. So I waited, and when winter came I did not go south. No. My world had changed. Now my world was the world of the Innuit. With this people, in that distant place, there was for me a peace of the heart, and a good feeling of the spirit. Yes, I was happy there.

The first year passed and a son was born to Nuljalik, and it seemed nothing could darken the happiness of our life together; yet even then there were little shadows flickering on the edge of things. So it must always be, perhaps, when a stranger comes to make his life with men of other customs and beliefs. He cannot be born again as one of them. As I became more and more familiar with the Innuit ways, I no longer admired everything they did . . . or thought. They seemed too much bound up with superstition. They had so many tabus, things that must or must not be done . . . a web of obstacles in a land where nature had placed obstacles enough before men. I could see no purpose worrying about a legion of devils and spirits that could exist only in imagination. But when I tried to treat such things as childish nonsense, it brought my wife such distress I was obliged to give lip service, at the least, to the pagan beliefs. Katelo was the wisest of all the Innuit and once I tried to make him see the foolishness of the people's fear of spirits. This is how he replied:

"In the land of the *Kablunait*—the white men—things may be as you say . . . but this is not the land of the Kablunait. I do not understand how it is in your land. You do not understand how it is here. We know what we know."

After that I tried to keep my impatience to myself and, in truth, it did not bother me so much. My life was very busy. I learned to spear the caribou at the river crossings and to be a good traveller over the winter wastes. I learned the lusty songs of the Innuit and I myself became something of a story-teller during the long nights when we clustered in the snowhouses and talked and sang the dark hours away. Seldom did I feel a desire to return south. What was there for me that I did not have with the Innuit? In

23

the great plains I had work, good friends, a wife and child.

Ah, yes, my friend, that was the happy time, and it lasted for three years . . . but, bear with me now, for what I have to tell has been a pain that half a century has never dulled.

In the autumn of the third year, I was sick and the shaman, Powhuktuk, came to my tent and sang magic songs. I got well, as I would have done in any case, but when I was back on my feet Powhuktuk warned me I must not hunt for as many days as I had been sick. He was a real ancient, Powhuktuk, with a face like dried fish skins and a voice as hard and shrill as a hawk's; and he knew how I felt about the beliefs his people held. He stood in front of me, outside my tent, and he shook his old bird-claw hands in my face and spit flew from his mouth, so determined was he to make me understand how serious this matter was.

"It is the kindness of Kaila, Mother of Life, that you are well," he wheezed at me. "So you must pay her back by not harming any of her children for twelve days and nights. If you kill anything it will be bad. You will bring evil here! Paija herself will come and make us pay!"

Paija, I knew about. She was believed to be the most cruel of all the spirits. To me it was nonsense, but I kept my counsel. I might also have kept the tabu, except it was late in the year and, because of my sickness, I did not have quite enough caribou in my caches. I knew the migrating herds might leave the plains before twelve days and I did not intend to let my woman and child go hungry in the long winter that stretched ahead. This I told myself . . . knowing all the same that if I ran short my neighbours would make good my needs. Yes, I knew that, but also I did not wish to be dependent for I was a young man filled with much pride. Or perhaps—how can I know now?—perhaps I wanted to find an excuse to break a foolish law . . . to *show* those people how little their superstitions meant to me.

On the ninth day of the tabu a big herd of deer came out of the north and began to cross the river a mile below our camp. They were the best of bucks—big, heavy, each carrying a blanket of fat three or four inches thick under his hide. They were also likely to be the *last* of the bucks for that year and so every hunter in our camp launched his kayak and flew downstream into the middle of the swimming herd.

I followed in my own kayak.

In the confusion and excitement of the slaughter, the men did not at first notice I was among them but then, one by one, they paused in the spearing, looked sideways at me and paddled away from the killing place. Before long I was alone there, my spear and right arm drenched with deer blood.

When I paddled home the camp was silent. Even the dogs were quiet. I saw no one as I walked up to my tent. When I told my wife of the hunt I had made, she too was silent, but late that night she woke me with her weeping and when I asked her why she cried, she would not speak. She did not need to, for I knew. I began to feel guilty—not on account of Paija but because I had brought fear into the hearts of the people.

Men do not often bear guilt easily and so I shouted harsh words at Nuljalik and called her a fool. Then I went to the tent of Katelo, and there were many people with him. I shouted at them too, calling them children and worse than children. Only Katelo answered and he waited until I had shouted myself out.

"Ayorama—it cannot be helped," he said. There was no anger in his voice. *"Eemah,* Saluk has done what he has done. Perhaps it will come to nothing."

His gentleness only angered me more. I went quickly to my own tent, but I did not sleep well for although Nuljalik tried to make no noise, I knew she wept the whole night through.

Winter set in soon after. Storm followed storm and for weeks we could hardly stir from the snowhouses. When at last there came a short period of calm and we could visit our distant meat caches, we found that a plague of wolverines had invaded the land and many caches had been ripped open and the meat stolen or spoiled. Then, a little time later, a crazed fox came into camp and the dogs set upon it and killed it, but not until many of them had been bitten. We had to kill those dogs for as you know the hydrophobia is a disease that cannot be stopped except by death.

These misfortunes were not unnatural, but it seemed there were too many of them. No one mentioned the breaking of the tabu in my presence, but I knew people were thinking about it and I became short tempered and grew harsh even with my own wife and child. One night when I insisted to Nuljalik that the wolverines were not devils but only animals, she replied, *"Kakwik,* the wolverine, is the servant of Paija."

Then, for the first time, I struck Nuljalik. I hit her hard with the flat of my hand and knocked her to the floor of the snowhouse. She did not cry but only went back to the work of sewing a new pair of boots for me.

As time went on, the wolverines grew bolder and began raiding caches within sight of our camp. The few dogs remaining to us would not attack them and we were losing meat we could not spare. In the darkness of the long nights the men of the camp would not even venture out to protect the caches. It seemed the fear of Paija was afflicting them all. So I took it on myself to protect the meat, and many were the black, frozen hours I spent tramping around the caches. Although I sometimes got a glimpse of one of the robbers, I did not manage to kill any of them and the loss of meat and fat went on.

Then one night when I was visiting the caches there came a pause in the wind and the grey curtain of ground drift stilled. There was a rift in the clouds and the white lights of the aurora shone brightly enough so I could see a fresh track in the hard snow before me. It was a single footprint, but it was huge. It was nearly as long as my forearm and its shape was almost like that of a human foot.

For a few moments my breath stopped and I was so frightened I could not move. I had heard many stories about Paija! It was said she was a giantess possessed of a single leg that grew out of the middle of her belly. It was said she visited human camps only by darkness, when the blizzards roared, clothed in nothing except her own coarse black hair. It was said that to see her was to die with a great hole ripped in your chest out of which Paija had torn the living spirit of her victim.

Although I believed none of this, the sight of that great footprint, before the clouds closed in and the wind whipped up the snow wraiths again, truly struck fear into my heart. I made for the shelter of the nearest snowhouse. It was Katelo's. When I scrambled in through the door tunnel it was to find many people crowded on the sleeping ledge in the yellow light of the fat lamps. They stared at me as if fearing what I might do or say. In that warm, lighted place

I shook off my own panic and when I had greeted the people I said:

"Look you. I have just come from the caches and I know who is robbing us of our meat. It is not the wolverines alone, it is a mightier beast. I have found the tracks of *Akla,* the giant brown bear."

Silence greeted my words and the faces before me seemed to shrink into themselves. In my anxiety to convince them of the truth of what I had seen, I went too far.

"Truly it is the bear!" I cried. "I have seen his tracks. I can show them to you. Like the tracks of a very big man!"

A young girl far back on the ledge screamed shrilly.

"Paija!" she wailed. "Paija is here!"

I stood there hearing nothing but the short, sharp breathing that comes with terror. At last Katelo spoke. He did not look at me.

"Akla does not walk in the winter, Saluk. In the winter he sleeps in his house under the snow."

It was what everybody knew . . . what I knew myself, only for the moment I had forgotten. Then I saw what a fool I had been. I began to understand what I had done.

It was late then to make amends, but I went back to my own snowhouse and took my wife in my arms and told her I had done wrong in breaking the tabu. As I tried to soothe her, I spoke of the strength of the white man's God and I told her that now I would call upon this God to protect the people from Paija. At first I spoke only to give her peace, but it came to me after awhile that if I could convince the Innuit of God's power then the wolverines would become only wolverines again; the print in the snow would belong to a bear that had somehow been roused

28

from its winter sleep; and the shadow of Paija, which was darkening the minds of the people, would vanish.

I jumped to my feet, picked up our child and, pulling Nuljalik after me, ran to Katelo's. The place was still crowded. The people were afraid to go to their own homes. The children whimpered and the women stared with faces rigid with fear. Ah, my friend, how it hurt to see them like that! Yes, and to know that the fault was my own!

Old Powhuktuk, the shaman, was there on the broad ledge with the rest. I spoke directly to him.

"Powhuktuk! You are a great *angeokok*, master of spirits, here in this land. Well then, hear me, for I am also an angeokok in the lands of the south. I too have the ear of great spirits. I too can command them to help me."

All eyes were on me and I turned slowly and looked into each of those faces.

"Listen, you people! I will call up *my* spirits, and they will do battle with Paija, and they will drive her away!"

Then I crossed myself and I, who had not been to mass for so many years, began to pray out loud. At first I only said meaningless phrases that did not come from the heart, but as the old familiar words rang in my ears some part of the faith of my childhood began to return. Soon I was praying passionately and I fell to my knees. Something of my passion seemed to pass to the watchers and they began to sway where they sat. My voice grew stronger as I chanted and I felt power within me. Something seemed to flow back and forth between me and the people. They began chanting too, in low, humming voices—ancient chants of the Innuit, making a background for my Christian prayers. . . .

It lasted for hours, until I was drained of my strength and soaking with sweat. The emotions that had gripped me were so strong, and so strange, that I was dazed, hardly knowing what I was doing. Katelo and Powhuktuk lifted me to a place on the ledge and one of the women began to serve soup from a pot hung over a lamp. That place was alive again. There was new life in those faces. Those men and women who had never reproached me for what I had done were going to believe I had been able to undo my mistake. They had faith.

All but one. Powhuktuk spoke out above the babble of talk and his old, whistling voice brought silence.

"Saluk! Maybe your spirits are strong. Are they strong enough? Have they indeed driven Paija away?"

I replied slowly and solemnly.

"*Imah!* Yes! She is gone! She will never return!"

There was another young man there that night —Onekwa, a good friend of mine, only recently married. Now he jumped off the ledge happily shouting that he was going to fetch his wife and father and mother from their snowhouse nearby. Katelo waved him on his way, telling him to go to all the houses and ask the people to come for a feast. Onekwa nodded and crawled out through the tunnel. I turned to look at Nuljalik who was trimming a lamp. She lifted her head, smiling at me with a face that was warm with the light of the lamp, and warmer still with the love she bore me . . . and then, from the darkness outside, there came a terrible cry!

How can I describe it? It was beyond mortal words for it held terror beyond anything mortal.

For one moment it was as if I saw before me the dreadful shape of Paija herself. The people were transfixed by that cry and it appeared that I alone

30

had the power of motion. There was a deer spear of Katelo's in a niche beside me. I grabbed it and made for the door, shouting, "Akla! The bear has got Onek-wa!"

My wife forestalled me. She flung herself against my legs so that we fell together to the hard-packed floor, and as we struggled her voice rose in a frenzied wail.

"Not Akla! Paija come for her gift! You will not go out!"

She fought like a demented thing and I had no time to be gentle with her. I caught her by her long black hair and flung her against the wall and again I plunged toward the doorway that loomed black before me.

I can see that dark tunnel mouth so clearly still . . . for it was the last thing I ever saw. Nuljalik had scrambled to her feet. She seized a fat lamp and flung it at my head. It missed me but the scalding oil ran down my brow into my eyes, and they instantly became twin sockets of fire. Dimly I heard my wife's voice, as if from a great distance.

"You *must* not look on her . . . you *will* not look on her!"

Then I was aware of nothing but the agony, and I rolled on the floor like an animal. I hardly felt my wife push past me as she thrust her way into the dark tunnel. . . .

André paused, and the pause lengthened. His hands gripped the edge of the table with such pressure that the old bones shone translucently through the yellowed skin. His sightless eyes were no longer wells of mystery. He was looking through them down the long years into the abyss of an igloo tunnel into which his woman had vanished.

31

Slowly his grip on the table relaxed. He folded his hands in his lap and calmly continued his story.

For many days I was in a delirium of pain, but I remember calling unceasingly for my wife. Nobody answered for a very long time, then one day I heard the voice of Katelo.

"Call no more for Nuljalik! Call no more for your wife! Paija has been here . . . and is gone with her gift."

Why they let me remain alive is a mystery to me. Yet I, who had no right to expect it, received kindness from them. They took my son from me, it is true, but I can believe he grew up to be a good man, one who lived according to the laws of his people. It was the right thing they did, and I did not resent it. As for me, there followed seven months of darkness in the new camp the people moved to.

On a day late in the summer I was lying alone in the small tent the Innuit had pitched for me when I heard a voice speaking Chipewyan. It was Denikazi, and with him was Father Danioux. The priest had at last come north to bring the light of God to the heathen Esquimaux. You may judge his surprise when he found me there; but he was friendly toward me and so for the first time I was able to unburden myself. He listened in silence to my tale, and when I had finished, he put his hand on my forehead.

"Ah, my son, you have sinned greatly. It was blasphemy for such a one as you to command God's help . . . you who had long ago forsaken Him. And it was a great sin to have even pretended to believe in the superstitions of these poor people. Yes, but harsh was the penance. To lose your wife to the bear because of her pagan beliefs, and to lose your sight because of that same heathen devil-worship, was indeed terrible. Truly you have suffered. But take comfort now for *le bon Dieu* is merciful. He will welcome you back and He will give you the opportunity to make amends for your sins. You will begin by helping me bring these poor children of darkness into the way of the Faith."

Instead of giving comfort, his words touched off madness in me. To him the sacrifice Nuljalik had made was clearly no more than the act of an ignorant animal. I sat up on the pile of skins and savagely flung his hand away.

"You lie!" I raged. "It was no bear! It was the devil-bitch, Paija, who slaughtered my wife!"

That violent rejection of God and priest might have led a lesser man to abandon me but, whatever his faults may have been, Father Danioux would not do such a thing. The next day, when I was calmer, he talked to me again and I repented of my rage and did not reject his desire to bring me back to the comfort of religion. But I refused to help him in his mission to the Innuit. I refused because I remembered Katelo's words when I challenged the beliefs of his people:

". . . this is not the land of the Kablunait . . . you do not understand how it is here. We know what we know."

I remembered, and I who had dealt a deep wound to those who had been so good to me would not wound them again. Perhaps the time might come when they would welcome the God of the white men . . . but that time was not yet.

I said as much to Father Danioux. Angrily and without my help he went ahead with his mission to the Innuit; and when that mission failed, he was convinced, doubtless with justice, that it was my stubbornness which had prevented him from bringing many heathen souls to the True Path.

Even so, when he and Denikazi departed they took me with them. After we reached Caribou, there was nowhere for me to go, so Father Danioux took me into the mission. Then he set himself the task of cleansing my soul.

Life slowly began to have meaning for me again as I determined to atone for what I had done, by serving God. Despite my blindness I made myself useful to Father Danioux, being willing to do all he asked of me . . . except one thing.

One thing alone I would not do. I would not condemn my wife and her people for what they believed. I would not disavow their beliefs. How could I do that? It would have been to make mockery of Nuljalik's death . . . of the gift she had made. No! Though he demanded it of me for the fifty years we were together, sometimes shouting that I was an unredeemed sinner and a heretic in my heart, I would not bend to his will.

That struggle between us remained unresolved until death stood beside him. His breathing had quieted and I knew that he lived only because of the faint warmth on the hand I laid on his face. It may be I felt rather than heard his last words:

". . . it would have been . . . a far greater sin . . . if you had denied her who gave you your life. . . ."

Stranger in Taransay

The village of Taransay straggles along a bleak piece of craggy shore on the outer Hebrides—those high-domed sentinels that guard the Scottish mainland coast from the driving fury of the Western Ocean. The few strangers who visit Taransay remember the acrid smell of peat smoke on the windswept hills, the tang of the dark local ale, and the sibilant patter of the Gaelic tongue spoken by the shepherds and fisher-men who gather during the long evenings under the smoke-stained ceiling of the Crofter's Dram.

It is the only public house for many miles, and it holds within its walls the beating heart of Taransay, together with many of its memories. Strange objects hang from the narrow ceiling beams or crowd the shelves behind the bar—remembrances of ancient wrecks, flotsam of the northern seas, the trivia of time. Amongst them is a collection of tiny figures delicately carved in white bone. These are ranged in the place of honour on a centre shelf where they catch the eye and stir the mind to wonderment. There are narwhals, long-beaked and leaping from an ivory sea; walrus thrusting tiny tusks through a miniature kayak; three polar bears snarling defiance at a human figure whose upraised arm holds a sliver of a spear; and a pack of arctic wolves poised in dreadful immobility over a slaughtered muskox.

There is an alien artistry about those carvings that never sprang from the imagination of an island shepherd, yet all were carved in Taransay. They are the work of a man named Malcolm Nakusiak who was a voyager out of time.

Nakusiak's odyssey began on a July day in the mid-1800s, under a basalt cliff in a fiord on the eastern shore of Baffin Island. To the score or so of people who lived there, it was known as *Auvektuk*—the Walrus Place. It had no name in our language for no white man had ever visited it although each year many of them, in stout wooden vessels, coasted the Baffin shores chasing the Bowhead whale.

These great whales were no part of men's lives at Auvektuk. For them walrus was the staff of life. Each summer when the ice of Davis Strait came driving south, the men of Auvektuk readied spears, harpoons and kayaks and went out into the crashing tumult of the Strait. On the grinding edges of the floes they stalked obese, ton-weight giants that were armoured with inch-thick hide, and armed with double tusks that could rend a kayak or a man.

Of all the Auvektuk hunters, few could surpass Nakusiak. Although not yet thirty years of age, his skill and daring had become legendary in his own

36

time. Young women smiled at him with particular warmth for Eskimo women do not differ from their sisters the world over in admiring success. During the long winter nights Nakusiak was often the centre of a group of men who chanted the chorus as he sang his hunting songs. But Nakusiak had another skill. He was blessed with fingers that could imbue carvings made of bone and walrus ivory with the very stuff of life. Indeed, life was a full and swelling thing for Nakusiak until the July day when his pride betrayed him to the sea.

On that morning the waters of the Strait were ominously shrouded with white fog. The hunters had gathered on the shore, listening to the ludicrous fluting voices of the first walrus of the season talking together somewhere to seaward. The temptation to go after them was great, but the risk was greater. Heavy fog at that time of the year was the precursor of a westerly gale and for a kayaker to be caught in pack ice during an offshore storm was likely to be fatal. Keen as they were for walrus meat, courageous as they were, these men refused the challenge. All save one.

Gravely ignoring the caution of his fellows, Nakusiak chose to wager his strength—and his luck—against the imponderable odds of the veiled waters. The watchers on the shore saw his kayak fade into obscurity amongst the growling floes.

With visibility reduced to about the length of the kayak, Nakusiak had great difficulty locating the walrus. The heavy fog distorted their voices and confused the direction, yet he never lost track of them and, although he had already gone farther to seaward than he had intended, he still refused to give it up and turn for home. He was so tautly concerned with the

37

hunt that he hardly noticed the rising keen of the west wind. . . .

Some days later, and nearly two hundred miles to the southeast, a Norwegian whaler was pounding her way southward through Davis Strait. The dirty, ice-scarred wooden ship was laden to her marks with oil and baleen. Her crewmen were driving her toward the hoped-for freedom of the open seas, all sails set and drawing taut in the brisk westerly that was the last vestige of a nor'west gale.

In the crow's nest the ice-watch swung his telescope, searching for leads. He glimpsed something on a distant floe off the port bow. Taking it to be a polar bear he bellowed a change of course to the helmsman on the poop. Men began to scurry across the decks, some running for guns while others climbed partway up the shrouds to better vantage points. The ship shouldered her way through the pack toward the object on the ice and the crew watched with heightened interest as it resolved itself into the shape of a man slumped on the crest of a pressure ridge.

The ship swung into the wind, sails slatting, as two seamen scampered across the moving ice, hoisted the limp body of Nakusiak in their arms and danced their way back from floe to floe, while a third man picked up the Eskimo's broken kayak and brought it to the ship as well.

The whalers were rough men, but a castaway is a castaway no matter what his race or colour. They gave Nakusiak schnapps, and when he was through choking they gave him hot food, and soon he began to recover from his ordeal on the drifting ice. All the same, his first hours aboard the ship were a time of bewilderment and unease. Although he had seen whaling ships in the distance, and had heard many barely credible stories from other Eskimos about the Kablunait—the Big Ears—who hunted the Bowhead, he had never before been on a ship or seen a white man with his own eyes.

He began to feel even more disturbed as the whaler bore steadily toward the southeast, completely out of sight of land, carrying him away from Auvektuk. He had been hoping the ship would come about and head north and west along the coast into the open water frequented by the Bowheads, but she failed to do so, and his efforts to make the Kablunait realize that he must go home availed him nothing. When the ship reached open water, rounded Kap Farvel at the south tip of Greenland and bore away almost due east, Nakusiak became frantic. Feverishly he began repairing his kayak with bits of wood and canvas given to him by the ship's carpenter, but he worked so obviously that he gave away his purpose. The newly patched kayak was taken from him and lashed firmly to the top of the after hatch where it was always under the eye of the helmsman and the officer on watch. The whalers acted as they did to save Nakusiak's life, for they believed he would surely perish if he put out into the wide ocean in such a tiny craft. Because he came of a race that accepted what could not be altered, Nakusiak ceased to contemplate escape. He had even begun to enjoy the voyage when the terrible winds of his own land caught up to him again.

The whaler was southeast of the Faeroe Islands when another ice-born nor'west gale struck her. She was a stout ship and she ran ably before it, rearing and plunging on the following seas. When some of her double-reefed sails began to blow out with the noise of cannon fire, her crew stripped her down to bare poles; and when the massive rollers threatened to poop her, they broke out precious cases of whale oil,

39

smashed them open and let the oil run out of the scuppers to smother the pursuing graybeards.

She would have endured the storm had not her mainmast shrouds, worn thin by too many seasons in the ice, suddenly let go. They parted with a wicked snarl and in the same instant the mainmast snapped like a broken bone and thundered over the lee side. Tethered by a maze of lines, the broken spar acted like a sea anchor and the ship swung inexorably around into the trough ... broached, and rolled half over.

There was no time to launch the whaleboats. The great seas tramped over them, snatching them away. There was barely time for Nakusiak to grab his knife, cut the kayak loose, and wriggle into the narrow cockpit before another giant comber thundered down upon the decks and everything vanished under a welter of water.

Washed clear, Nakusiak and the kayak hung poised for a moment on the back of a mountainous sea. The Eskimo held his breath as he slipped down a slope so steep it seemed to him it must lead to the very bowels of the ocean. But the kayak was almost weightless, and it refused to be engulfed by the sucking seas. Sometimes it seemed to leap free and, like a flying fish, be flung from crest to crest. Sometimes it flipped completely over; but when this happened, Nakusiak, hanging head down beneath the surface, was able to right his little vessel with the twisting double paddle. He had laced the sealskin skirt sewn to the cockpit coaming so tightly around his waist that no water could enter the vessel. Man and kayak were one indivisible whole. The crushing strength of the ocean could not prevail against them.

The bit of arctic flotsam, with its human heart, blew into the southeast for so long a time that Nakusiak's eyes blurred into sightlessness. His ears became impervious to the roar of water. His muscles cracked and twisted in agony. And then, as brutally as it had begun, the ordeal ended.

A mighty comber lifted the kayak in curling fingers and flung it high on the roaring shingle of a beach where it shattered like an egg. Although he was half stunned, Nakusiak managed to crawl clear and drag himself above the storm tide line.

Hours later he was awakened from the stupor of exhaustion by the cries of swooping, black-backed gulls. His vision had cleared, but his brain remained clouded by the strangeness of what lay around him. The great waves rolled in from the sounding sea but nowhere on their heaving surface was there the familiar glint of ice. Flocks of sea birds that were alien both in sound and form hung threateningly above him. A massive cliff of a dull red hue reared high above the narrow beach. In the crevices of the cliff outlandish flowers bloomed, and vivid green turf such as he had never seen before crested the distant headlands.

The headlands held his gaze for there was something on them which gave him a sense of the familiar. Surely, he thought, those white patches on the high green places must be scattered drifts of snow. He stared intently until fear shattered the illusion. The white things moved! They *lived!* And they were innumerable! Nakusiak scuttled up the beach to the shelter of a water-worn cave, his heart pounding. He knew only one white beast of comparable size—the arctic wolf—and he could not credit the existence of wolves in such numbers . . . if, indeed, the things he had seen were only wolves, and not something even worse.

For two days Nakusiak hardly dared to leave the cave. He satisfied his thirst with water dripping from the rocks, and tried to ease his hunger with oily

41

tasting seaweed. By the third day he had become desperate enough to explore the cliff-locked beach close to his refuge. He had two urgent needs: food ... and a weapon. He found a three-foot length of driftwood and a few minutes' work sufficed for him to lash his knife to it. Armed with this crude spear his courage began to return. He also found food of sorts; a handful of shellfish and some small fishes that had been trapped in a tidal pool. But there was not enough of these to more than take the edge off his growing hunger.

On the morning of the fourth day he made his choice. Whatever alien world this was that he had drifted to, he would no longer remain in hiding to endure starvation. He determined to leave the sterile little beach and chance whatever lay beyond the confining cliffs.

It was a long and arduous climb up the red rock wall and he was bone weary by the time he clawed his way over the grassy lip to sprawl, gasping for breath, on the soft turf. But his fatigue washed out of him instantly when, not more than a hundred paces away, he saw a vast assemblage of the mysterious white creatures. Nakusiak clutched the spear and his body became rigid.

The sheep, with the curiosity characteristic of members of their family, were intrigued by the fur-clad figure on the rim of the cliff. Slowly the flock approached, led by a big ram with black, spiralled horns. Some of the ewes shook their heads and bleated, and in this action the Eskimo saw the threat of a charge.

The sheep bleated in a rising chorus and shuffled a few feet closer.

Nakusiak reached his breaking point. He charged headlong into the white mob, screaming defiance as he came. The sheep stood stupidly for a moment, then wheeled and fled, but already he was among them, thrusting fiercely with his makeshift spear.

The startled flock streamed away leaving Nakusiak, shaking as with a fever, to stare down at the two animals he had killed. That they were mortal beings, not spirits, he could no longer doubt. Wild with relief he began to laugh, and as the sound of his shrill voice sent the remaining sheep scurrying even farther into the rolling distance, Nakusiak unbound his knife and was soon filling his starving belly with red meat—and finding it to his taste.

The strange scene under the pallid Hebridean sky had been witnessed by the gulls, the sheep . . . and by one other. Atop a ridge a quarter mile inland a sharp-faced, tough-bodied man of middle age had seen the brief encounter. Angus Macrimmon had been idly cleaning the dottle from his pipe when his practised shepherds' glance had caught an unaccustomed movement from the flock. He looked up and his heavy brows drew together in surprise as he saw the sheep converging on a shapeless, unidentifiable figure lying at the edge of the cliff. Before Macrimmon could do more than get to his feet he saw the shape rise—squat, shaggy and alien—and fling itself screaming on the flock. Macrimmon saw the red glare of blood against white fleece and watched the killer rip open a dead sheep and begin to feed on the raw flesh.

The Hebrideans live close to the ancient world of their ancestors, and although there are kirks enough on the Islands, many beliefs linger on that owe nothing to the Christian faith. When Macrimmon watched the murder of his sheep, he was filled not only with anger but with dread, for he could not credit that the thing he saw was human.

Cursing himself for having left his dog at home,

the shepherd went for help, running heavily toward the distant village. He was breathless by the time he reached it. Armed with whatever they could find, a dozen men were soon gathered together, calling their dogs about them. Two of them carried muzzle-loading shotguns while another carried a long-barrelled military musket.

The day was growing old when they set out across the moors, but the light was still clear. From afar the shepherds saw the white flecks that were the two dead sheep. Grouped close, they went forward cautiously until one of them raised an arm and pointed, and they all saw the shaggy thing that crouched beside one of the sheep.

They set the dogs on it.

Nakusiak had been so busy slicing up meat to sundry in the morning that he did not notice the approaching shepherds until the frenzied outcry of the dogs made him look up. He had never before seen dogs like these and he had no way of knowing that they were domestic beasts. He sprang to his feet and stood uncertainly, eyes searching for a place of refuge. Then his glance fell on the grim mob of approaching shepherds and he sensed their purpose as surely as a fox senses the purpose of the huntsmen.

Now the dogs were on him. The leader, a rangy black-and-brown collie, made a circling lunge at this strange-smelling, strangely clad figure standing bloody handed beside the torn carcasses. Nakusiak reacted with a two-handed swing of the spear-haft, striking the bitch so heavily on the side of her head that he broke her neck. There was a hubbub among the shepherds, then one of them dropped to his knee and raised the long musket.

The remaining dogs closed in again and Nakusiak backed to the very lip of the cliff, swinging the shaft to keep them off. He lifted his head to the shepherds and in an imploring voice cried out: "*Inukuala eshui-nak!* It is a man who means no harm!"

For answer came the crash of the gun. The ball struck him in the left shoulder and the force of the blow spun him around so that he lost his balance. There was a shout from the shepherds and they rushed forward, but they were still a hundred yards away when Nakusiak stumbled over the cliff edge.

There was luck in the thing, for he only fell free a few feet before bringing up on a rocky knob. Scrabbling frantically with his right hand he managed to cling to the steep slope and slither another yard or so past a slight overhang until he could lie, trembling and spent, on a narrow ledge undercut into the wall of rock.

When the men joined the hysterical dogs peering over the cliff edge, there was nothing to be seen except the glitter of waves on the narrow beach far below and the flash of gulls disturbed from their resting places.

The shepherds were oddly silent. They were hearing again that despairing cry, instantly echoed by the shot. Whatever the true identity of the sheep killer might be, they knew in their hearts that he was human, and the knowledge did not sit easily with them.

They shifted uncomfortably until the man who had fired spoke up defiantly.

"Whatever 'twas, 'tis gone now surely," he said. "And 'tis as well, for look you at the way it tore the sheep and killed the dog!"

The others glanced at the dead dog and sheep, but they had nothing to say until Macrimmon spoke.

"Would it not be as well, do you think, to make a search of the beach?"

"Ach, man, don't be daft!" the gunner replied irritably. " 'Twould be the devil's own job to gang down there . . . and for what? If that thing was alive when it fell, then 'tis certain dead enough now. And if 'twas never alive at all . . ." He let the sentence lie unfinished.

Calling the dogs the shepherds moved homeward over the darkening moors, and each one wrestled with his doubts in silence.

There was no policeman at Taransay, and no one offered to carry a message to the nearest constable across the mountains to distant Stornaway. Macrimmon put the feelings of all the men into words when he was being questioned about the event by his wife and daughters.

"What's done is done. There's no good to come from telling the wide world what's to be found on the moors, for they'd no believe it. Best let it be forgotten."

Yet Macrimmon himself could not forget. During the next two days and nights he found himself haunted by the memory of that alien voice. Up on the inland moors sloping to the mountain peaks, the wind seemed to echo it. The cry of the gulls seemed to echo it. It beat into the hard core of the man and would not be silenced and, in the end, it prevailed.

On the third morning he stood once more at the edge of the cliff . . . and cursed himself for a fool. Nevertheless, that dour and weatherbeaten man carefully lowered himself over the cliff edge. His dog wheened unhappily but dared not follow as his master disappeared from view.

The tide was driving out and the shingle glistened wetly far below him, but the shepherd did not look down. He worked his way skilfully, for in his youth he had been a great one at finding and carrying off the eggs of the cliff-nesting gulls. However, he was no youth now and before he had descended halfway he was winded and his hands were cut and bruised. He found a sloping ledge that ran diagonally toward the beach and he was inching his way along it when he passed close to a late-nesting gannet. The huge bird flung herself outward, violently flailing the air. A wing struck sharply against Macrimmon's face and involuntarily he raised a hand to fend her off. In that instant the shale on which his feet were braced crumbled beneath him and he was falling away toward the waiting stones.

Unseen on the cliff top the dog sensed tragedy and howled.

The dog's howl awakened Nakusiak from fevered sleep in the protection of the little cave which had been his first sanctuary. Here, on a bed of seaweed, he lay waiting for his body to heal itself. His swollen shoulder throbbed almost unbearably but he stolidly endured, for it was in his nature to endure. All the same, as he waited for time to work for him, he was conscious that there was nothing ahead in this alien world but danger and ultimate destruction.

When the dog's howl woke him, Nakusiak shrank farther into the recesses of his cave. His good hand clutched the only weapon left to him . . . a lump of barnacle-encrusted rock. He lifted it and held it poised as the rattle of falling stones mingled with a wailing human shout outside his cave.

His heart beat heavily in the silence that followed. It was a silence that reminded Nakusiak of how it is when an ermine has cornered a ground squirrel in a rock pile and waits unseen for the trapped beast to venture out. Nakusiak was aware of anger rising above his pain. Was he not *Inuk*—a Man—and

47

was a man to be treated as a beast? He changed his grip on the rock, then, with a shout of defiance, stumbled out of his sanctuary into the morning light.

The sun momentarily blinded him and he stood tensely waiting for the attack he was sure would come. There was no sound . . . no motion. The glare eased and he stared about him. On a thick windrow of seaweed a few yards away he saw the body of a man lying face down, blood oozing from a rent in his scalp.

Nakusiak stared at this, his enemy, and his heart thudded furiously as the inert body seemed to stir, and mumbled sounds came from its mouth. In an instant Nakusiak was standing over the shepherd, the lump of rock raised high. Death hovered over Angus Macrimmon, and only a miracle could have averted it. A miracle took place. It was the miracle of pity.

Nakusiak slowly lowered his arm. He stood trembling, looking down at the wounded man and the trickle of blood from the deep wound. Then with his good arm Nakusiak gripped the shepherd, rolled him over, and laboriously dragged his enemy up the shingle to the shelter of the cave.

A search party found the dog on the cliff edge the next morning and guessed grimly at what had happened. But the searchers only guessed a part of it. When a couple of hours later six of them, all well armed, reached the beach in a fishing skiff, they were totally unprepared for what they found.

A thin curl of smoke led them directly to the cave. When they came to peer fearfully into the narrow cleft, guns at the ready, their faces showed such baffled incredulity at the scene before them that Macrimmon could not forbear smiling.

"Dinna be frighted, lads," he said from the seaweed mattress where he lay. "There's none here but us wild folk and we'll no eat you."

Inside the cave a small driftwood fire kindled by Nakusiak with Macrimmon's flint and steel burned smokily. The shepherd's head was bound with strips of his own shirt, but his bruised back with its broken ribs was covered with the fur parka that had been on the back of the sheep stealer not long since. Beside him, staring uneasily at the newcomers, Nakusiak sat bare to the waist, hugging his wounded shoulder with his good arm.

The Eskimo glanced nervously from Macrimmon's smiling face to the blob of heads crammed into the cave entrance, then slowly he too began to smile. It was the inexpressibly relieved grin of one who has been lost in a frightful void and who has come back into the land of men.

For many days Nakusiak and Macrimmon lay in adjoining beds in the shepherd's cottage while their wounds healed. Macrimmon's wife and daughters gave the Eskimo care and compassion, for they acknowledged their debt to him. For his part, he entertained them with songs in Eskimo, at which the good wife muttered under her breath about "outlandish things," but smiled warmly at the stranger for all of that.

As he was accepted by the Macrimmons, so was he accepted by the rest of the villagers, for they were kindly people and they were also greatly relieved that they did not have to bear the sin of murder. Within a few weeks the Eskimo was being referred to with affection by all and sundry as "the queer wee laddie who came out of the sea."

Nakusiak soon adjusted to the Hebridean way of life, having accepted the fact that he would never be able to return to his own land. He learned to speak the language, and he became a good shepherd, a superb hunter of sea fowl and grey seals, and a first-rate fisherman as well. Three years after his arrival at Taransay, he married Macrimmon's eldest daughter and started a family of his own, taking the Christian name of Malcolm, at the insistence of the young local clergyman who was one of those who particularly befriended him. During the long winter evenings he would join the other men at the Crofter's Dram and there, sitting before the open fire, would whittle his marvellous little carvings as a way of describing to his companions the life he had known in the distant land of the Innuit.

So Nakusiak, the man who had come so far in space and time from the Walrus Place to find a strange destiny in an alien world, lived out his life in Taransay. But it was no exile's life. Long before he died at the end of the century and was buried in the village churchyard, he had become one with the people of that place; and his memory remains a part of their memory still.

One summer afternoon in our time, a young man who is Nakusiak's great-grandson knelt to read the inscription written by the Eskimo's clergyman friend and carved into one of the twin stones that stand over the graves of Malcolm and his wife. There was pride in the young man's face and in the set of his shoulders as he read the words aloud:

Out of the sea from what lands none can tell,
This stranger came to Taransay to dwell.
Much was he loved who so well understood
How to return for evil a great good.

The Iron Men

As I sat in the doorway of my tent watching Hekwaw
at work, my glance travelled from the quick motions
of his lean hands, sending a knife blade gleaming over
white wood, to his rapt face. Black hair hung long
and lank over his brow, shadowing his eyes.

Dreaming over his task, he seemed neither to
see nor hear the world around him—a world of rolling
tundra, of looming hills, of rushing rivers and still
lakes; a world of caribou, white wolves, black ravens
and a myriad birds. The world that we, in our ig-
norance, chose to call the Barrenlands. It was Hekwaw's world but for the moment he was unaware
of it, intent on giving new life to a memory out of another age.

The long arctic sun was lying on the rim of the
horizon before he rose and came toward me carrying
the product of memory. It was a thing made of antler
bone, black spruce and caribou sinew . . . and it had

no place upon those northern plains. It was a crossbow, a weapon used by the Scythians in Asia Minor three thousand years ago and one that dominated the medieval battlefields of Europe until the age of gunpowder.

Some days earlier Hekwaw had been recalling stories from the ancient times of his people and he had spoken of a weapon I did not recognize. I questioned him until he drew a picture of it in the sand. I could not believe what he showed me, for it seemed impossible that his ancestors, isolated in the central arctic, could have discovered a weapon known to no other native American people. I asked him if he could make one of the weapons and he nodded. Now the crossbow was a reality.

Laying an unfeathered wooden bolt in the groove, he drew back the sinew string with both hands and lodged it in a crossways slit. On the shadowed river a red-throated loon dipped and swam. There was a sudden, resonant vibration on the still air. The bolt whirred savagely over the river and the loon flashed its wings in a dying flurry.

Hekwaw lowered the bow, placed it carefully beside him and squatted on his heels to light his stained old soapstone pipe. He did not wait for my questions but began a tale which had been called back to life across many centuries by the vibrant song of the crossbow.

Ai-ya! But this is a weapon! It came to us in distant times but I keep the memory of it because my fathers' fathers were men to whom it was given to remember. So it is that I can speak of the Innuhowik.

They were beings who seemed more than human, yet death could fell them. They were bearded, but their beards were not black like those of the God-

52

bringers—they were yellow and sometimes brown and looked as bright as copper. The eyes of some were brown also, but most were of the colour of the eastern sky just before sunrise, or the deep ice of the winter lakes. Their voices boomed and rumbled, and they spoke no words my people understood.

We never knew what land they came from, only that it lay eastward beyond salt waters which they travelled over in boats many times the length of a kayak.

In those days my people lived, as they had always lived, far inland and so they did not witness the arrival of the Innuhowik. The tents of my forbears stood along the shores of *Innuit Ku*, River of Men, which flows north out of the forests. My people avoided the forests for these belonged to the *Itkilit*, the Indians as you call them. In spring when the caribou migrated north out of their lands, the Itkilit sometimes followed, and when they came upon one of our camps there would be fighting. Afterwards they would withdraw into the shelter of the trees. We feared them, but the tundra plains were ours by right, as the forests were theirs by right, and so our southernmost camps stood only a few days' journey from the place where Innuit Ku emerges from the shadows of the trees.

One late-summer day when the leaves of the dwarf willows were already darkening, a young boy lay on the crest of a hill close to the most southerly Innuit camp. It was his task to give warning if the canoes of the Itkilit should appear. When he saw something moving far to the south he did not wait to be sure what it was. He came running like a hare over the rocky plain and his cry pierced into the skin tents of the families who lived at that place.

It was past noon and the men were mostly resting

53

in the cool tents, but at the sound of the boy's cry they ran out into the blazing light. Women clutched their babies and quickly led the older children into the broken hills beyond the River.

The people had chosen the site of that camp with care. A little distance to the south of it the River roared through a narrow gorge, tossing great plumes of spray high into the air. Neither canoe nor kayak could pass through unless it stayed close to the cliffs on the western side. And men lying on top of these western cliffs could look directly down upon the only safe channel. It was to this gorge that the Innuit men hurried when the boy gave the alarm. Beside each man was a pile of frost-shattered rocks, jagged edged and as heavy as one man could lift. These were the best weapons we could muster against the Itkilit, for in those times my people had not good bows because the only wood available to us was of a kind too weak and too soft.

The men atop the cliff had not long to wait before something came into sight far up the River. As it plunged toward them they stared fearfully, but they were perplexed too. It was a boat they saw—not a canoe—and one such as no Innuit had ever imagined. It was as long as three kayaks, as broad as the length of a man, and built of thick wooden planks. The beings it carried were stranger still. All save one sat with their backs to the front of the boat and pulled at long paddles set between wooden pins. There were eight of them, sitting in pairs. The ninth stood in the back facing the rest and holding another long paddle thrust out behind. He held the gaze of my people for he wore a shining metal cap on his head and under it his face was almost hidden by a long yellow beard. Polished iron sheets on his breast caught reflections from the swift waters and sent lights into the eyes of the men on the cliffs.

These strange ones were almost upon the Innuit, but my people were so bewildered they did not know how to act. Were these *men* below them? Or spirits? If they were spirits they could not be killed. They *could*, however, be angered, then there would be no way of knowing what they might do.

The big wooden boat swept into the gorge and was steered into the western channel by the tall man at the stern whose bellowing voice could be heard even above the roar of the waters. From the cliffs high above, my people watched . . . and did nothing, and the strangers passed on down the River.

As the Innuit began to rise to their feet, one of them yelled, and they all looked where he pointed. Three long, bark canoes had appeared upriver, and this time there was no doubt who came into our lands. They were Itkilit, dressed in scraped hides and wearing the faces of death, and driving their canoes as swiftly as wolves racing after a deer.

There was barely time for my people to snatch up the sharp rocks lying beside them. As the canoes flew past below, they came under a hail of boulders that smashed bark boats and men's bones. Two of the canoes broke apart like the skulls of rabbits under the blows of an axe.

The River was red that day; but from out of the spray of the gorge, one canoe emerged. The Innuit men ran to the shore, tossed their swift kayaks into the stream and gave chase.

Great falls block the River only a few miles downstream from the gorge, and it was toward the falls that the last canoe, holed by stones and with some of its men wounded, was being driven. When the funnelling current above the falls was reached, the Itkilit saw death ahead and knew death was behind them. At the last moment they turned out of the current and drove their sinking canoe ashore. They leapt up the bank toward a ridge of rocks from whose shelter they hoped to defend themselves from the Innuit.

They did not reach that ridge. It was already held by the iron-clad strangers who had also been warned by the current and by the roar of falling water and had gone to the shore. These strange ones rose up from behind the rocks of the ridge and charged down upon the Itkilit roaring like bears, thrusting with great long knives, and slashing with iron axes. Only a few Itkilit got back to the River. They flung themselves into it and were swept over the falls.

The strangers—they whom we later called Innuhowik, Iron Men—stood watching the kayaks where they hovered in the current. Perhaps my people seemed as terrifying to their eyes as they had seemed to ours, but they were brave. One of them came slowly to the shore carrying no weapon in his hands. At his approach the kayaks nervously moved out of the backwater and away from the land. The yellow-bearded leader of the Innuhowik came to the water's edge, and my people wondered at his size for he stood a head taller than any of them. They watched as he drew a short knife from his belt and held it out, handle first, toward the kayakers.

It was a man named Kiliktuk who paddled cautiously toward the spot and, reaching out his long, double-bladed paddle, touched the handle of the knife. The stranger smiled and laid the knife on the paddle blade so Kiliktuk could draw it to him without touching shore.

Soon all the kayaks were beached and the men who were my forefathers were crowded around the

Innuhowik fingering their tools and weapons. It was clear the strangers were not ill-disposed to the Innuit, so they were brought back to the camp. Far into that night the song-drums sounded while Innuit and Innuhowik sat together by the fires and feasted on caribou meat and fish. It is remembered that the strangers ate like men—like hungry men—and that they looked at our women with the eyes of men.

As to what happened after, the stories speak of many things. They tell especially of the strength of the Innuhowik, and of the wonderful tools and weapons they possessed. These were mostly of iron, which was unknown to the Innuit except as hard, heavy stones which sometimes fell from the skies.

After they had been in the camp for a few days, the Innuhowik began asking questions by means of drawings in the sand, and by signs, and the people understood that they wished to know if Innuit Ku led to the sea in the east. When they had been made to know that it did not, but led instead to the northern seas from which the ice seldom passes, they became unhappy. They talked with one another in loud voices, but at last came to an agreement and let us understand they wished to remain with us for a time.

We were glad to have them stay. They soon gave up wearing their own clothing of thick cloth and metal plates and put on the soft caribou-skin garments our women made for them. When the cold weather began they even put aside their horned iron caps which made them look like muskox bulls.

The Innuhowik knew many secret things. They could make fire by striking iron on rock and they had small blue stones that could tell them where the sun was even though the sky was black with clouds. But although they had much wisdom, there were many things in our land which were strange to them. We taught each other, and perhaps it was they who had the most to learn.

Their leader's name was Koonar. He could carry whole carcasses of caribou for many miles. He could split the skull of even the great brown bear when he wielded his long iron blade. His mind was just as strong, and in only a little time he could understand and speak our tongue. From Koonar's lips my people heard the story of how the Innuhowik came to our River. It was told that they sailed out of the northeast in their long wooden ships until they reached the coast of the sea which lies far to the east of us. Some of them stayed there guarding their ships while others took smaller boats and went inland up the rivers, though what it was they sought we never learned.

Koonar's boat went far south into unknown lands and travelled upon lakes and rivers running through the forests. But one night there was trouble with the Itkilit, and they fought, and some of the Innuhowik perished, as did many of the Itkilit. Koonar turned back but found his old way now barred by the Itkilit and so the Innuhowik followed new rivers north, hoping to be able to turn east to the shores where the long ships waited. When they were five days' travel to the south of the first Innuit camps, they came upon two tents of Itkilit and surprised the people in them, killing all except a young boy who escaped and carried word to other Itkilit camps. Then Koonar and his men were pursued into our land as I have already told.

Koonar lived in Kiliktuk's tent, where also lived Airut who was Kiliktuk's daughter. She was a fine young woman with full, round cheeks and a laughing voice. She had been married once but her man had been killed when his kayak was holed on a rapid in the River. Kiliktuk hoped Airut would seem good in

Koonar's sight so that Koonar might become a son in that tent. Yet Koonar, alone of his men, seemed not to desire a woman, and so he did not take Airut though she was willing.

One day in the month when the snows come, Koonar went to a cache near the deer crossing place to bring back some meat stored there. He was returning with two whole gutted carcasses on his shoulders when he slipped and fell among the rocks with such force that one of his thigh bones was shattered. He was carried into Kiliktuk's tent with pieces of bone sticking out of the flesh, and even his own men believed he would die. He was sick for a long time; and it may be that he lived only because Airut refused to let death take him away, and because Kiliktuk who was a great shaman could command the help of the spirits.

Koonar recovered but he never walked freely again nor did he regain his great strength, for it seemed the injury he had suffered had eaten into his heart. Truly he was changed, for now it came about that the hopes of Kiliktuk were realized. Koonar took Airut as his wife, even as his men had all taken wives, and after that my people believed the Innuhowik would stay forever in the camps of the Innuit.

The people were wrong. When the snows were thick on the land and the rivers were solidly frozen, the Innuhowik gathered in a big snowhouse the people had built for them and spent many days talking together. What all that talk came to in the end was that the Innuhowik decided to forsake their women and go away from the land of my people. They had made up their minds to travel eastward over the tundra plains, using some of our dogs and sleds.

My people were not willing that the Innuhowik should do this, for they needed their dogs and they were also angry on behalf of the women. It seemed it would come to a fight, until Koonar stepped in. He said if my people would assist the Innuhowik to go, he himself would remain and all the gifts he could make would be ours.

Do you wonder why he agreed to stay? My people wondered too. Perhaps he believed his injuries would make him a burden to his fellows; or perhaps it was because the woman, Airut, was with child.

In the worst time of winter, when the blizzards rule the land, the eight Innuhowik left our camps, driving dog sleds eastward in search of the salt sea and their own big ships. No word was ever heard of them again, not even by our cousins, the sea people, who live along the coasts. I think that in the dark depths of the winter nights their magic failed them and they perished.

So now the tale of the Innuhowik becomes the tale of Koonar, of Airut, and of the children she bore. First was the boy Hekwaw, whose name I bear, born in the spring. A year later Airut had a girl child who was called Oniktok, but afterwards she had no more children. Koonar seemed content with his life, even though he was so crippled he could hardly leave his tent or his snowhouse. The other men of the camp hunted the meat that fed Koonar and his family, but they were glad to do this because Koonar was well liked. He did not laugh as much as he had done when his own men were still with us, and he spent many hours playing Innuhowik games. He taught these to his son, and one of them was still played in my own grandfather's time. Many small squares were marked out on the snow or on a piece of deer hide, and each man had a number of stones . . . but now that game is forgotten.

Kiliktuk was the man closest to Koonar, since both were shamans who knew many magical things and understood each other's minds. Koonar would often talk of things he had seen in distant places. Sometimes he told of great battles on land and sea fought with such weapons that men's blood flowed like spring freshets. It was remembered that, when he spoke of such things, his face would become terrible and most people were afraid to remain in his presence even though such talk of great killings of men could not easily be believed.

Things went well in the many camps along the River until the child, Hekwaw, was in his eighth year and had become a very promising boy and a source of much pride to his father. After the snows began that autumn, Kiliktuk decided that a journey must be made south to cut trees for new sleds, kayak frames, tent poles and other wooden things that were needed. In earlier times this had been considered a dangerous venture, one to be made only when a large number of Innuit from many camps could band together for protection in case the Itkilit attacked the wood gatherers. But since the Itkilit had suffered so heavily at the gorge and the Killing Falls, it was thought they would not now be anxious to fight.

Because of his crippled leg, Koonar could not leave the camps in order to teach Hekwaw, his son, the ways of men on the land, so Kiliktuk had become the boy's teacher. Now he asked that Hekwaw accompany the wood-gathering party in order that he might learn the nature of the southern country. Koonar loved his son and wished him to become a foremost man, so he did not oppose this. The boy took his place on Kiliktuk's long sled, and a big party of men, some women and other boys set off to the south. They passed through the country of little sticks to the end of a big lake stretching far into the forests. Here they made camp.

Each morning thereafter the men drove south on the ice of the lake to where good timber grew on its shores. Before dark they would return to the travel camp where the women would greet them with trays of hot soup and boiled meat. At first some men stayed at the camp during the day to guard it, but when no signs of Itkilit were seen these men went also to help with the cutting.

On the sixth day, while the Innuit men were far down the lake, a band of Itkilit came running on snowshoes out of the small woods near the camp. When the Innuit men returned again in the evening, they found three women and three boys, Hekwaw among them, dead in the snow.

Kiliktuk and his companions did not pursue the Itkilit into the thick cover of the forests, knowing they would be helpless against the long bows, spitting their arrows from hiding. They were afraid that the slaughter of their women and children was planned to draw them into an ambush. So they wrapped the remains of the dead ones in caribou skins, loaded the sleds, and started north.

The sounds of their lamentings were heard in the river camps even before the dog teams were seen. It is remembered that when Kiliktuk entered Koonar's igloo he took an iron knife Koonar had given him and thrust it partway into his own chest, inviting Koonar to drive it home into his heart.

The fury of Koonar at the loss of his son was of a kind unknown to my people. It was of a kind unknown in our land. Koonar did not lament his dead, as my people did; he burned and roared in the grip of madness, and so terrifying was he that none dared come near him for the space of many days and nights. Then he grew silent . . . silent and cold, with a chill more dreadful than his fury. At last he ordered the people to bring him muskox horns, the best and hardest dry wood, plaited caribou sinews, and some other things.

He worked in his snowhouse for three days and when he was done he held in his hand the father of this bow which I have made—although what I have done is but the crude work of a child compared to what Koonar wrought.

For a long time after that he ordered the lives of the people in the camp as if they were no more than dogs. He drove each hunter to make a crossbow. If a man did not make it well enough, Koonar struck him and forced him to do it again. It is unthinkable for one of us to strike another, for to do so is to show that you are truly a madman; yet the people endured Koonar's madness, for their awe of him was the awe one has of a devil.

When each man had a crossbow and a supply of bolts, Koonar dragged himself out of the snowhouse and made them set up targets and practise shooting, day after day. Although it is not in my people's nature to give themselves in this way to such a task, they were afraid to resist.

With the coming of the long night which is the heart of winter, Kiliktuk, obeying Koonar's will, chose the ten best marksmen and ordered them to prepare dogs and gear for a long journey. Six teams were hitched to six sleds and the chosen men left the camps, heading south along the frozen river. Kiliktuk was in the lead, and on his sled lay Koonar, well wrapped in muskox robes against the brittle cold.

It is told how these men boldly drove into the forests, Koonar having banished both fear and caution from their hearts. For seven days they drove

63

southward among the trees, and in the evening of the seventh day they came in sight of the smoking tents of a big band of Itkilit upon a lake shore.

The Innuit would have preferred to draw back and wait for dawn before attacking, but Koonar would allow no delay. The sleds spread out and were driven at full speed across the intervening ice straight into the heart of the Itkilit camp. They came so swiftly, the Itkilit dogs hardly had time to howl an alarm before the sleds halted in a line and the Innuit men jumped off, bows in hand.

Many of the Itkilit came spilling out of their tents without even stopping to seize their own weapons, for they could not believe they would be attacked so boldly. They were met by the whine and whirr and thud of the bolts.

Many Itkilit died that night. The Innuit would not have harmed the women and children but Koonar demanded that everyone who could be caught be killed. When the slaughter was over, Koonar ordered the tents of the Itkilit burned down so that those who had escaped into the forests would die of starvation and frost.

While the flames were still leaping, the Innuit turned their teams northward. They drove with hardly a pause until the trees began to thin and the plains stretched ahead.

Only then did they make camp. Koonar was so exhausted that he could not move from his sled where he lay with eyes closed, singing strange songs in a voice that had lost most of its strength. When Kiliktuk tried to give him a drink of meat soup he thrust it aside, spilling it on the snow. It is remembered that there was no joy in that camp. Too much blood had been shed and there was darkness in the hearts of the men of my people.

At dawn the sleds drove north again, but when they were almost in sight of the home camps Kiliktuk's sled turned aside from the trail. He motioned the others forward, bidding them carry the news of the battle.

Late that night a man stepped out of his snowhouse at the home camp to relieve himself and saw something that made him shout until everyone in the camp came outside. To the north a tongue of fire thrust upward as if to join the flickering green flames of the spirit lights. The long roll of snow-covered hills by the Killing Falls emerged briefly from the darkness. The people were still watching in astonishment when a sled came swiftly into camp from northward. On it rode Kiliktuk ... and he was alone.

He was asked many questions, but neither then nor later did he tell the people how the last of the Innuhowik departed. Only to his grandson, the son of Koonar's daughter, did he tell that tale. That child also was called Hekwaw and he was the father of my father's fathers, and it was through them that I heard how Kiliktuk drove Koonar down the River to the place where the Innuhowik's old boat was still cached among the rocks. It was from them I heard how Kiliktuk tenderly placed Koonar in that boat and piled bundles of dry willow scrub around him. Then Kiliktuk put the flint and steel in Koonar's hands and parted from the stranger who had become his son.

Kiliktuk drove away as he had been ordered to do, and when he looked back, flames were already lifting above the boat. So the last of the Innuhowik went from our lands to that place of warriors where, he had told us, his people go at the end of their time.

There followed many years and many generations during which my people prospered because of

65

the gift of this bow. We no longer feared the Itkilit and in our pride and strength went against them. We drove them south into the forests for such a distance that, after a time, they were hardly even remembered. Our camps spread over the whole width and breadth of the plains.

But in the time of my grandfather's grandfather, the strangers returned.

This time they came not to our country but to the forested lands in the south, and there they made friends with the Itkilit. They did not wear iron on their breasts or on their heads, and they were not called Innuhowik. They were *your* people, who are called *Kablunait*. The Kablunait brought gifts to the Itkilit, and foremost of these was the gun.

Then the Itkilit considered what we had done to them in times they had never forgotten.

They came north out of the forests again, first in small bands and then in hundreds, and Koonar's gift failed us. They killed us from great distances with their guns and they roamed so widely over our lands that my people had to flee north almost to the coasts of the frozen seas.

It seemed as if the guns brought by the Kablunait would mean an end to my people, and so it might have happened. But one summer the Itkilit failed to appear on the plains; and as summer followed summer and they still failed to return, my people began to move slowly south and recover their land.

The Itkilit stopped coming against us because they were dead in their thousands; dead from a fire that burned in their bodies, rotting the flesh so they stank like old corpses while life still lingered within them. This we know, for that fire, which was another gift from the Kablunait, afterwards swept out over the plains and my people also died in their thousands.

Now the Itkilit are no more than a handful scattered through the dark shadows of the forests; and the wide country where my people once dwelt is nearly empty of men.

So it ends. . . . But this bow I hold in my hand is where it began.

Darkness had fallen and the fire was nearly out. Hekwaw stirred the coals until the fire was reborn under the touch of the night wind. His face was turned from me as he dropped the crossbow onto the flames, and I could barely hear his words:

"Take back your gift, Koonar. Take it back to the lands of the Innuhowik and the Kablunait . . . its work here is done."

Two Who Were One

After death carried the noose to Angutna and Kipmik, their memory lived on with the people of the Great Plains. But death was not satisfied and, one by one, he took the lives of the people until none was left to remember. Before the last of them died, the story was told to a stranger and so it is that Angutna and Kipmik may cheat oblivion a little while longer.

It begins on a summer day when Angutna was only a boy. He had taken his father's kayak and paddled over the still depths of the lake called Big Hungry until he entered a narrow strait called Muskox Thing. Here he grounded the kayak beneath a wall of looming cliffs and climbed cautiously upward under a cloud-shadowed sky. He was hunting for *Tuktu*, the caribou, which was the source of being for those who lived in the heart of the tundra. Those people knew of the sea only as a legend. For them seals, walrus and whales were mythical beasts. For them the broad-antlered caribou was the giver of life.

Angutna was lucky. Peering over a ledge he saw three caribou bucks resting their rumbling bellies on a broad step in the cliffs. They were not sleeping, and one or other of them kept raising his head to shake off the black hordes of flies that clung to nostrils and ears, so Angutna was forced to crawl forward an inch or two at a time. It took him an hour to move twenty yards, but he moved with such infinite caution that the bucks remained unaware of his presence. He had only a few more yards to crawl before he could drive an arrow from his short bow with enough power to kill.

Sunlight burst suddenly down through the yielding gray scud and struck hot on the crouched back of the boy and the thick coats of the deer. The warmth roused the bucks and one by one they got to their feet. Now they were restless, alert, and ready to move. In an agony of uncertainty Angutna lay still as a rock. This was the first time he had tried to stalk Tuktu all by himself, and if he failed in his first hunt he believed it would bode ill for his luck in the years ahead.

But the burst of sunlight had touched more than the deer and the boy. It had beamed into a cleft in the cliffs overhanging the ledge where it had wakened two sleeping fox pups. Now their catlike grey faces peered shortsightedly over the brilliant roll of the lake and the land. Cloudy black eyes took in the tableau of the deer and the boy; but in their desire to see more, the pups forgot the first precept of all wild things—to see and hear but not to be seen or heard. They skittered to the edge of the cleft, shrilling a mockery of the dog fox's challenge at the strange beasts below.

The bucks turned their heavy heads and their ears flopped anxiously until their eyes found the pups scampering back and forth far over their heads. They continued to watch the young foxes, and so they did not see the boy move rapidly closer.

The hard twang of the bow and the heavy thud of an arrow striking into flesh came almost together. The deer leapt for the precipitous slope leading to the lake, but one of them stumbled, fell to his knees, and went sliding down on his side. In a moment Angutna was on him. The boy's copper knife slipped smoothly between the vertebrae in the deer's neck, and the buck lay dead.

The curiosity of the pups had now passed all bounds. One of them hung so far out over the ledge that he lost his balance. His hind legs scrabbled furiously at the smooth face of the rocks while his front feet pushed against air. The rocks thrust him away and he came tumbling in a steep arc to pitch into the moss almost at Angutna's feet.

The pup was too stunned to resist as the boy picked him up by the tail. Angutna put a tentative finger on the small beast's head, and when it failed to snap at him he laughed aloud. His laughter rang over the hills to the ears of the mother fox far from her den; it speeded the flight of the two surviving bucks, and rose to the ears of a high-soaring raven.

Then the boy spoke to the fox:

"*Ayee!* Kipmik—Little Dog—we have made a good hunt, you and I. Let it be always this way, for surely you must be one of the Spirits-Who-Help."

That night in his father's skin tent Angutna told the tale of the hunting. Elder men smiled as they listened and agreed that the fox must indeed be a good token sent to the boy. Tethered to a tent pole, the pup lay in a little grey ball with his ears flat to his head and his eyes tightly shut, hoping with all his small heart that this was only a dream from which he would wake to find solace at the teats of his mother.

Such was the coming of the white fox into the habitations of men. In the days that followed, Angutna shared most of his waking hours with Kipmik who soon forgot his fears; for it is in the nature of the white fox to be so filled with curiosity that fear can be only a passing thing.

While the pup was still young enough to risk falling into the lean jaws of the dogs that prowled about the camp, he was kept tethered at night; but during the days, fox and boy travelled the land and explored the world that was theirs. On these expeditions the pup ran freely ahead of the boy over the rolling plains and hills, or he squatted motionless on the precarious deck of a kayak as Angutna drove the slim craft across the shining lakes.

Boy and fox lived together as one, and their thoughts were almost as one. The bond was strong between them for Angutna believed the fox was more than a fox, being also the embodiment of the Spirit-Who-Helps which had attached itself to him. As for Kipmik, perhaps he saw in the boy the shape of his own guardian spirit.

The first snows of the year came in late September and soon after that Kipmik shed the sombre grey fur of youth and donned the white mantle of the dog fox. His long hair was as fine as down and the white ruff that bordered his face framed glistening black eyes and the black spot of his nose. His tail was nearly as long and as round as his body. He was small compared to the red foxes who live in the forests, but he was twice as fleet and his courage was boundless.

During the second winter they spent together,

Angutna came of age. He was fifteen and of a strength and awareness to accept manhood. In the time when the nights were so long they were almost unbroken, Angutna's father spoke to the father of a young girl named Epeetna. Then this girl moved into the snowhouse of Angutna's family and the boy who was now a man took her to wife.

During the winters life was lived without much exertion in the camps of the barrenland people for the deer were far to the south and men lived on the fat and meat they had stored up from the fall slaughter. But with the return of the snowbirds, spring and the deer came back to the plains around the Big Hungry and the camps woke to new and vigorous life.

In the spring of the first year of his marriage, Angutna went to the deer-hunting places as a full-fledged hunter. With him went the white fox. The two would walk over the softening drifts to reach rocky defiles that channelled the north-flowing deer. Angutna would hide in one of the ravines while the fox ran high up on the ridges to a place where he could overlook the land and see the dark skeins of caribou approaching the ambush. When the old doe leading a skein approached the defile, she would look carefully around and see the little white shadow watching from above. Kipmik would bark a short greeting to Tuktu, and the herd would move fearlessly forward believing that, if danger lurked, the fox would have barked a cry of alarm. But Kipmik's welcoming bark was meant for the ears of Angutna, who drew back the arrow on the bent bow and waited.

Angutna made good hunts during that spring and as a result he was sung about at the drum dances held in the evenings. The fox was not forgotten either, and in some of the songs the boy and the fox were called the Two Who Were One, and that name became theirs.

In the summer, when the deer had passed on to the fawning grounds far to the north, the fox and the boy sought other food. The Two Who Were One took the kayak down the roaring rivers that debouched over the scarred face of the plains, seeking the hiding places of the geese that nested in that land. After midsummer the adult geese lost their flight quills and had to stay on the water, and at such times they became very shy. The kayak sought out the backwaters where the earthbound geese waited in furtive seclusion for the gift of flight to return.

While Angutna concealed himself behind rocks near the shore, Kipmik would dance on the open beach, barking and squealing like a young pup. He would roll on his back or leap into the air. As he played, the geese would emerge from their hiding places and swim slowly toward him, fascinated by this peculiar behaviour in an animal they all knew so well. They had no fear of the fox for they knew he would not try to swim. The geese would come closer, cackling to one another with necks outstretched in amazement. Then Angutna's sling would whir and a stone would fly with an angry hiss. A goose would flap its wings on the water and die.

It was an old trick Kipmik played on the geese, one used by foxes since time began . . . but only Kipmik played that game for the benefit of man.

So the years passed until there were two children in the summer tent of Angutna—a boy and a girl who spent long hours playing with the soft tail of the fox. They were not the only young to play with that white brush. Every spring, when the ptarmigan

73

mated on the hills and the wild dog foxes barked their challenges as an overtone to the sonorous singing of the wolves, unrest would come into the heart of the fox that lived in the houses of men.

On a night he would slip away from the camp and be gone many days. When he returned, lean and hungry, Angutna would feed him special tidbits and smilingly wish good luck to the vixen secreted in some newly dug den not far away. The vixen never ventured into the camp, but Kipmik saw to it that she and her pups were well fed, for Angutna did not begrudge the fox and his family a fair share of the meat that was killed. Sometimes Angutna followed the fox into the hills to the burrow. Then Angutna might leave a fresh fish at its mouth, and he would speak kindly to the unseen vixen cowering within. "Eat well, little sister," he would say.

As the years slipped by, stories of the Two Who Were One spread through the land. One of them told of a time when Angutna and his family were camped alone by the lake called Lamp of the Woman. It was a very bad year. In midwinter there was an unbroken month of great storms and the people used up all the meat stored near the camp but the weather was too savage to permit the men to travel to their more distant caches. The people grew hungry and cold, for there was no more fat for the lamps.

Finally, there came a day without wind. Angutna hitched up his team and set out for a big cache lying two days' travel to the west. The dogs pulled as hard as their starved muscles would let them while the fox, like a white wraith, flitted ahead, choosing the easiest road for the team. The sled runners rasped as if they were being hauled over dry sand, for the temperature stood at fifty or sixty degrees below freezing.

On the second day of the journey the sun failed to

show itself and there was only a pallid grey light on the horizon. After a while the fox stopped and stared hard into the north, his short ears cocked forward. Then Angutna too began to hear a distant keening in the dark sky. He tried to speed up the dogs, hoping to reach the cache, which lay sheltered in a deep valley, before the storm broke. But the blizzard exploded soon after, and darkness fell with terrible swiftness as this great gale, which had swept a thousand miles south from the ice sea, scoured the frozen face of the plains. It drove snow before it like fragments of glass. The drifting granules swirled higher and higher, obscuring the plodding figures of man, fox and dogs.

Kipmik still moved at the head of the team but he was invisible to Angutna's straining, snowcaked eyes, and many times the anxious white shadow had to return to the sled so that the dogs would not lose their way. Finally the wind screamed to such a pitch that Angutna knew it would be madness to drive on. He tried to find a drift whose snow was firm enough for the making of a snowhouse, but there was none at hand and there was no time to search. Turning the sled on its side facing the gale, he dug a trench behind it with his snowknife—just big enough for his body. Wrapping himself in his robes he rolled into the trench and pulled the sled over the top of the hole.

The dogs curled abjectly nearby, noses under their tails, the snow drifting over them, while Kipmik ran among them snapping at their shoulders in his anxiety to make them continue on until some shelter was found. He gave up when the dogs were transformed into white, inanimate mushrooms. Then the fox ran to the sled and burrowed under it. He wormed in close, and Angutna made room so that he might share the warmth from the little body beside him.

For a day and a night nothing moved on the white face of the dark plains except the snow ghosts whirling before the blast of the gale. On the second day the wind died away. A smooth, curling drift shattered from within as Angutna fought free of the smothering snows. With all the haste his numbed body could muster, he began probing the nearby drifts seeking the dogs who were sealed into white tombs from which they could no longer escape by themselves.

He had little need of the probe. Kipmik ran to and fro, unerringly sniffing out the snow crypts of the dogs. They were all uncovered at last, and all were alive but so weak they could barely pull at the sled.

Angutna pressed on. He knew that if no food was found soon, the dogs would be finished. And if the dogs died, then all was lost, for there would be no way to carry the meat from the cache back to the camp. Mercilessly Angutna whipped the team on, and when the dogs could no longer muster the strength to keep the sled moving, he harnessed himself into the traces beside them.

Just before noon the sun slipped over the horizon and blazed red on a desolate world. The long sequence of blizzards had smoothed it into an immense and shapeless undulation of white. Angutna could see no landmarks. He was lost in that snow desert, and his heart sank within him.

Kipmik still ran ahead but for some little while he had been trying to swing the team to a northerly course. Time after time he ran back to Angutna and barked in his face when the man persisted in trudging into the west. So they straggled over that frozen world until the dogs could go no farther. Angutna killed one of the dogs and fed it to the others. He let them rest only briefly, for he was afraid a new storm would begin.

The sun was long since gone and there were no stars in the sky when they moved on; therefore, Angutna did not notice as, imperceptibly, Kipmik turned the team northward. He did not notice until late the next morning when the dawn glow showed him that all through the long night they had been travelling into the north.

Then Angutna, who was a man not given to rage, was filled with a terrible anger. He believed it was all finished for him and his family. He seized his snowknife from the sled and with a great shout leapt at the fox, his companion of so many years.

The blow would have sliced Kipmik in two but, even as he struck, Angutna stumbled. The blade hissed into the snow and the fox leapt aside. Angutna stayed on his knees until the anger went from him. When he rose to his feet he was steadfast once more.

"*Ayorama!*" he said to the fox who watched him without fear. "It cannot be helped. So, Little Pup, you will lead us your way? It is a small matter. Death awaits in all directions. If you wish, we will seek death to the north."

It is told how they staggered northward for half a day, then the fox abandoned the man and the dogs and ran on ahead. When Angutna caught up to Kipmik it was to find he had already tunnelled down through the snow to the rocks Angutna had heaped over a fine cache of meat and fat in the fall.

A year or so later a great change came to the world of the plains dwellers. One winter day a sled drove into the camps by the Big Hungry and a man of the sea people came into the snowhouses. Through many long nights the people listened to his wondrous

77

tales of life by the salt water. They were particularly fascinated by his accounts of the wonders that had been brought to that distant land by a white man come out of the south. Their visitor had been commissioned by the white man to acquaint the plains people with the presence of a trading post on the eastern edge of the plains, and to persuade them to move close to that post and to trap furs for trade.

The idea was much talked about and there were some who thought it would be a good thing to go east for a winter, but most of the people were opposed. By reason of his renown as a hunter, Angutna's opinions carried weight and one night he spoke what was in his mind.

"I think it is to be remembered that we have lived good lives in this land, knowing little evil. Is it not true that *Tuktoriak* has fed and clothed us from before the time of the father's fathers? *Eeee!* It is so. And if we turn from the Deer Spirit now to seek other gifts, who can say what he may do? Perhaps he will be angry and speak to his children, the deer, and bid them abandon our people. And then of what value would be the promises made by this man on behalf of the Kablunait? . . . Those promises would be dead sticks in our hands."

So spoke Angutna, and most agreed with him. Still, when the stranger departed, there were two families who went with him. These returned before the snows thawed in the spring and they brought such wealth as a man could hardly credit: rifles, steel knives, copper kettles and many such things.

But they also brought something they did not know they were bringing.

It was a sickness that came into men's lungs and squeezed the life from their bodies. It was called the Great Pain and it flung itself on the plains people like a blazing wind. In one season it killed more than half of those who lived in that land.

Panic struck many of the survivors who, believing the land was now cursed, fled to the east to seek help from the white man. From him they learned a new way of life, becoming trappers of fur and eaters of white man's food. And, instead of Tuktu, the beast they now pursued was Terriganiak—the white fox. During all time that had been, the plains people had known the white fox as a friend in a land so vast and so empty that the bark of the fox was often the only welcoming sound. Since time began, foxes and men had shared that land and there had been no conflict between them. Now men turned on Terriganiak and lived by the sale of his skin.

For a time Angutna and a few other men and their families tried to continue living the old life in the old places, but hunger came more often upon them and one autumn the deer failed to appear at all. Some said this was because of the great slaughter of deer resulting from the new rifles in the hands of all northern people, Indian and Innuit; but Angutna believed it was due to the anger of Tuktoriak. In any event, the last few people living on the inland plains were forced to follow those who had already fled to the east and become trappers of fox.

When the survivors of that long trek came to the snowhouses which stood a few miles away from the house of the trader at the mouth of the River of Seals, they expected to be greeted with warmth and with food, for it had always been the law of the land that those who have food and shelter will share with those who have not.

Disappointment was theirs. White foxes, too, were scarce that winter and many traps stood empty. Those people who had chosen to live by the fox were

79

nearly as hungry as the people who journeyed out of the west.

Angutna built a small snowhouse for his family, but it was a dark place filled with dark thoughts. There was no fuel for the lamps and almost no fuel for the belly. Angutna, who had once been such a great hunter, was now forced to live on the labours of others because, even if he had so wished, he could not have trapped foxes. He could not have done so because Terriganiak was his Spirit-Who-Helps and, for him, the lives of all foxes were sacred. Other men went to their traps and, when they were lucky, caught foxes whose pelts they bartered for food. Sometimes a portion of that food was given to Angutna's wife; but Angutna had nothing to give in return.

The new way of life was as hard for Kipmik as for Angutna. The fox who had always been free now lay, day and night, tethered to a stick driven into the floor of the snowhouse. All around that place steel traps yawned for his kind and there were many men with rifles who, to help feed their families, would not have hesitated to put a bullet through him, for although Kipmik was growing old, his pelt was still thicker, softer and longer than that of any fox that had ever been seen before.

As the winter drew on, the remaining foxes deserted that part of the country and then hunger was the lot of all who had tried to live by the fox. There were no more gifts to the family of Angutna, who had himself become so emaciated that he could do little but sit like a statue in his cold house, dreaming of other times, other days. Sometimes his gaze would fix on the curled ball of white fur that was Kipmik, and his lips would move, but silently, for he was addressing a plea to the Spirit-Who-Helps. Sometimes the fox would raise its head and stare back into the eyes of the man, and perhaps he too was pleading . . . for the freedom that once had been his.

The trader heard about the fabulous fox who lived in the houses of men and one day he drove his dogs to the camps of the people to see for himself whether the stories were true. He entered Angutna's snowhouse, and as soon as he saw Kipmik curled up on the floor he wished to possess that magnificent pelt.

It distressed him to see the big, staring eyes and the swollen bellies of Angutna's children. He felt pity for the people who were starving that winter. But what could he do? He did not own the food that lay in his storehouse. It belonged to the company that employed him, and he could not part with a pound unless there was payment in fur.

Angutna greeted the visitor with a smile that tautened the skin that was already stretched too tightly over the broad bones of his face. Even though he be in despair, a man must give a good greeting to those who visit his house. It was otherwise with the fox. Perhaps he smelled the death stink from the skins of so many of his kind this stranger had handled. He pulled away to the side of the snowhouse as far as his tether would reach and crouched there like a cat facing a hound.

The white man spoke of the hard times that lay on the people; of the shortage of foxes and the absence of deer. Then he turned to look at Kipmik again.

"That is a fine fox you have there. I have never seen better. If you will sell it to me, I can pay . . . as much as three sacks of flour and, yes, this I can do, ten, no, fifteen pounds of fat."

Angutna still smiled, and none knew the thoughts that swirled behind the masked face. He did not answer the white man directly, but spoke instead of trivial things while he wrestled with himself in his mind: food . . . food enough to ensure that his wife and children would live until spring. Perhaps he even believed his Spirit-Who-Helps had something to do with the miraculous hope the white man extended. Who will know what he thought?

The trader knew better than to say anything more about Kipmik, but when he went outside to his waiting sled he ordered his Eskimo helper to take a small bag of flour into Angutna's snowhouse. Then he returned to his trading post at the mouth of the River of Seals.

That night the woman, Epeetna, made a small fire of willow twigs in the tunnel entrance and she and her children ate unleavened bread made of flour and water. She passed a cake of it to Angutna where he sat unmoving on the sleeping ledge, but he did not taste it. Instead he threw it to the fox. Kipmik bolted it down, for he too was starving. Then Angutna spoke, as it seemed, to himself.

"This is the way it must be."

Epeetna understood. The woman let her hair loose so that it hung down over her face. The acrid smoke from the fire clouded the four figures sitting on the high ledge. The small flames gave hardly enough light for Angutna to see what he was doing, but his fingers needed no light as he carefully plaited the Noose of Release.

When it was finished, Angutna slipped Kipmik's tether, and the fox leapt up to the ledge and stood with its paws braced against the chest of the man— free once again. The black eyes were fixed on the eyes of the man, in wonder perhaps, for the fox had never seen tears in those eyes before. Kipmik made no move when the noose fell over his neck. He made no move until Angutna spoke.

"Now, Little Pup, it is time. You will go out onto the plains where the deer wait our coming."

And so Kipmik passed into that country from which nothing returns.

Next morning when the trader opened his door he found the frozen pelt of the fox suspended from the ridge of his porch by a strangely plaited noose. The pelt swayed and spun in the breath of the wind. The trader was delighted, but he was uneasy too. He had lived in that land long enough to know how little he knew. He wasted no time ordering his helper to load the promised food on a sled and take it to the snowhouse of Angutna.

The payment was received by Epeetna. Angutna could not receive it, for the Noose of Release was drawn tight at his throat. He had gone to join the one he had lost.

His grave still stands on the bank of the River of Seals. It is no more than a grey cairn of rocks with the decayed weapons of a hunter scattered among the quiet stones. Inside the grave lies Angutna, and beside him lies the fox who once lived in the houses of men.

The two are still one.

The Blood in Their Veins

Barely visible from Gene Lushman's rickety dock at the mouth of Big River, Anoteelik stroked his kayak to seaward on the heaving brown waters of Hudson Bay. Vanishing, then reappearing on the long, slick swells, the kayak was so distant it might have been nothing more than an idle gull drifting aimlessly on the undulating waters.

I had helped Anoteelik prepare for that journey. Together we had carried the skin-wrapped packages of dress goods, food and tobacco down from Lushman's trading shack. Then the squat, heavy-bodied Eskimo, with his dreadfully scarred face, lashed the cargo to the afterdeck and departed. I watched him until the bright flashing of his double-bladed paddle was only a white flicker against the humped outlines of a group of rocky reefs lying three miles offshore.

This was the third time I had seen Anoteelik make his way out of the estuary to the farthest islet on the sombre rim of the sea but it was the first time I understood the real reason behind his yearly solitary voyage.

Gene Lushman, barrenland trapper and trader, had first drawn my attention to him three years earlier.

"See that old Husky there? Old Ano . . . tough old bugger . . . one of the inland people and queer like all of them. Twenty years now, every spring soon as the ice clears, Ano, he heads off out to the farthest rock, and every year he takes a hundred dollars of my best trade goods along. For why? Well, me son, that crazy old bastard is taking the stuff out there to his dead wife! That's true, so help me God! He buried her there . . . far out to sea as there was a rock sticking up high enough to hold a grave!

"Father Debrie, he's tried maybe a half dozen times to make the old fellow quit his nonsense. It has a bad influence on the rest of the Huskies—they're supposed to be Christians, you know—but Ano, he just smiles and says: 'Yes, Father,' and every spring he turns in his fox skins to me and I sell him the same bill of goods, and he takes it and dumps it on that rock in the Bay."

It was the waste that bothered and puzzled Gene. Himself the product of a Newfoundland outport, he could not abide the waste . . . a hundred dollars every spring as good as dumped into the sea.

"Crazy old bastard!" he said, shaking his head in bewilderment.

Although he had traded with the Big River people for a good many years, Gene had never really bridged the gap between them and himself. He had learned only enough of their language for trade purposes and while he admired their ability to survive in their harsh land he had little interest in their inner lives, perhaps because he had never been able to stop

85

thinking of them as a "lesser breed." Consequently, he never discovered the reason for Anoteelik's strange behaviour.

During my second year in the country, I became friendly with Itkut, old Anoteelik's son—indeed his only offspring. Itkut was a big, stocky man still in the full vigour of young manhood; a man who laughed a lot and liked making jokes. It was he who gave me my Eskimo name, *Kipmetna*, which translates as "noisy little dog." Itkut and I spent a lot of time together that summer, including making a long boat trip north to Marble Island after walrus. A few days after our return, old Ano happened into Itkut's tent to find me struggling to learn the language under his son's somewhat less-than-patient guidance. For a while Ano listened to the garbled sounds I was making, then he chuckled. Until that moment the old man, with his hideously disfigured face, had seemed aloof and unapproachable, but now the warmth that lay hidden behind the mass of scar tissue was revealed.

"Itkut gave you a good name," he said smiling. "Indeed, the dog-spirit must live in your tongue. *Ayorama*—it doesn't matter. Let us see if we can drive it out."

With that he took over the task of instructing me, and by the time summer was over we had become friends.

One August night when the ice fog over the Bay was burning coldly in the long light of the late-setting sun, I went to a drum dance at Ano's tent. This was forbidden by the priest at Eskimo Point, who would send the R.C.M.P. constable down to Big River to smash the drums if he heard a dance was being held. The priest was a great believer in an ever-present Devil, and he was convinced the drums were the work of that Devil. In truth, these gatherings were song-feasts at which each man, woman or child took the drum in turn and sang a song. Sometimes it was an ancient song from far out of time, a voice from the shadowy distances of Innuit history; or perhaps it might be a comic song in which the singer made fun of himself. Often it was the story of a spectacular hunting incident; or it might be a song of tragic happenings and of the spirits of the land.

That night Itkut sang a song of the Hunting of Omingmuk, the muskox. As the story unwound, Ano's face came alight with pride—and with love.

Toward dawn people began to drift away and Ano suggested we walk to the shore and have a smoke. Flocks of plover, grey and ephemeral in the half light, fled shrilling before us, and out on the dim wastes of the sea spectral loons yapped at one another.

Ano's face was turned to the sea.

"I know you wonder at me, Kipmetna, yet you look at this torn face of mine and your questions are never heard. You watch as I make my spring journey out to the rock in the sea and your questions remain silent. That is the way also with my People. Tonight, perhaps because Itkut sang well and brought many memories to me from a long time ago, I would tell you a story."

Once there was a woman, and it was she who was my belly and my blood. Now she waits for me in that distant place where the deer are as many as the stars.

She was Kala, and she was of the Sea People, and not of my People who lived far from the sea on the great plains where no trees grow. But I loved her beyond all things in the sea or on the land. Some said I loved her too much, since I could never find the strength to share her, even with my song-cousin, Tanugeak. Most men respected my love and the *angeokok*, Mahuk, said that the sea-mother, Takanaluk Arnaluk, was pleased by the love I had for my wife.

My mother was Kunee and my father was Sagalik. I was born by the shore of Tulemaliguak, Lake of the Great Bones, far west of here, in the years when the camps of the inland people were almost emptied of life by the burning breath of the white man's sickness. My father died of it soon after my birth.

I was born in the late summer months, and Kunee, my mother, was dead before autumn. Then I was taken into the childless tent of Ungyala and his wife Aputna. They were not young people. Once they had lived very far to the south but their camps too had been stricken by the sickness and they had fled north. They too had been burned by the flame in the lungs, and their sons and daughters had died.

Soon after they took me into their tent, Ungyala and Aputna made ready to flee again, for there were not enough people left in our camps even to bury the dead. So we three went west . . . far off to the west into a land where the Innuit had never lived for fear of the Indians who sometimes came out of the forests into the plains. The deer were plentiful in that place and we lived very well while I grew toward the age of a man and learned to hunt by myself and to drive the long sled over the hard-packed snow.

All the same, it was a lonely land we had come to. There were not even any Indians—perhaps they too had been burned by the plague. We saw no *inukok*, little stone men set on the hills to tell us that other men of our race had travelled those long, rolling slopes. It was a good land but empty, and we hungered to hear other voices.

In the winter of the year when I became *angeut-nak*, almost a man, the blizzards beat upon us for a very long time. Ungyala and I had made good kills of deer in the autumn so we three did not suffer; yet we longed for the coming spring, the return of the deer and the birds. We yearned for the voices of life, for the voices we heard were of wind and, sometimes I thought, of those spirits who hide in the ground.

In the month when the wolves begin to make love there came a break in the storms. Then I, in the pride of my youth and filled with a hunger I could not yet name, decided to make a journey to the north-west. I said I hoped to kill muskox and bring fresh meat to the camp. Ungyala agreed to my going, though he was not very willing for he was afraid of the lands to the northwest. I took seven dogs and drove the ko-matik over the snow-hidden hills for three days, and saw no living thing. That land was dead, and my heart was chilled, and only because I was stubborn and young did I go on.

On the fourth day I came to the lip of a valley, and as I began to descend my lead dog threw up her head. In a moment the dogs were plunging into soft snow, the traces all tangled, and all of them yelling like fiends. I stopped them and walked cautiously forward until I could look down into the flat run of a gulley that lay sheltered by walls of grey stone. There was movement down there. It was *kakwik*, the wolverine, digging with his slashing front claws into the top of what looked like a drift. I ran back to my team and tried to unleash a few of the dogs so they could chase him, but now they were fighting each other; and before I could free them, kakwik was gone, lumbering up the long slope and over the rocks.

I kicked at the dogs, jumped on the sled, and drove headlong into the gulley; but when I slowed past the place where kakwik had duḡ, my heart went out of the chase.

He had been digging into the top of a buried snowhouse.

Ungyala believed that no men lived to the west and north of our land, yet here was a house. The door tunnel was snowed in and drifts had almost buried the place. I took my snow probe and slid it into a crack between blocks in the roof. It went in so easily I could tell the inside was empty of snow.

I grew cautious and more than a little afraid. The thought came that this might be the home of an *Ino*, a dwarf with knives where his hands should be. Yet the thought that this might instead be the home of true men gave me courage.

With my snowknife I cut a hole in the dome . . . squeezed through it and dropped to the floor. As my eyes grew used to the gloom, I saw that this had been a shelter for men . . . only now it was a tomb for the dead.

There were many bones lying about and even in that dim light I could see that not all had belonged to deer or muskox. One was a skull with black hair hanging down over gleaming white bone where the flesh of the cheeks had been cut away with a knife.

I was about to leap up to the hole in the roof and drag myself out of that terrible place when I saw a shudder of movement under a pile of muskox robes at the back of the sleeping ledge. I was sure something terrible crouched there in the darkness and I raised my snowknife to strike, and fear was a sliver of ice in my belly.

But it was no devil that crawled painfully out from under that pile of rotting hides.

Once, I remember, I found the corpse of a fawn wedged in a deep crevice among some great rocks. It had been missed by the ravens, foxes and wolves and, because it was autumn, the maggots had not eaten the meat. It had dried into a bundle of bones bound around with skin.

The girl who lay helpless before me on the ledge of the snowhouse looked like that fawn. Only her eyes were alive.

Although I was young, and greatly afraid, I knew what I must do. There was a soapstone pot on the floor. I slid the blade of my knife into the flesh of my left arm and let the hot blood flow into the bowl.

Through the space of one day and night I fed the thing I had found with the blood from my veins. Drop by drop was she fed. In between feedings I held her close in my arms under a thick new robe I had fetched from my sled, and slowly the warmth from my body drove the chill from her bones.

Life came back to her but it was nearly three days before she could sit up at my side without aid. Yet she must have had hidden strength somewhere within her for later that day when I came back into the snowhouse after feeding my dogs, all the human bones on the floor, to the last fragment, had vanished. She had found strength, even though death still had his hands on her throat, to bury those things under the hard snow of the floor.

On the fifth day she was able to travel so I brought her back to Ungyala's camp and my parents-by-right took her in and were glad she had come. Neither one made any comment when I told how I had found her and what else I had found in the snow-house. But later, when Ungyala and I were on a journey away from the camp picking up meat from an autumn cache, he spoke to me thus:

"Anoteelik, my son, this person has eaten the flesh of the dead . . . so much you know. Yet until you too have faced death in the way that he came to this girl, do not judge of her act. She has suffered enough. The spirits of those she has eaten will forgive her . . . the living must forgive her as well."

The girl quickly recovered her youth—she who had seemed beyond age—and as she grew fat she grew comely and often my heart speeded its beat when she was near. She spoke almost no words except to tell us her name was Kala and that her family, who were Sea People, had come inland from the north coast in the fall to hunt muskox.

It was not until the ravens returned that one day when we men were far from the camp, she broke into speech to my mother-by-right. Then she told how the family dogs had died of the madness which is carried by foxes and wolves, and how, marooned in the heart of the dark frozen plains, her parents and brother had followed the Snow Walker. She told how she also had waited for death until hunger brought its own madness . . . and she began to eat the flesh of the dead. When she finished her tale she turned from my mother-by-right and cried, "I am unworthy to live!" She would have gone out into the night and sought her own end had my mother not caught her and bound her and held her until we returned.

She was calmer by the next day, but she asked that we build her a snowhouse set apart from the camp, and we followed her wish. She lived alone there for many days. Aputna took food to her and talked to her, but we two men never saw her at all.

It was good that spring came so soon after, for spring is the time for forgetting the past. The deer streamed back into our land. The ptarmigan mated and called from the hills, and the male lemmings sought out the females deep in the moss.

The snowhouses softened under the sun and then

Kala came back and lived with us in the big skin tent that we built. She seemed to have put out of mind the dark happenings of the winter, and she willingly helped with the work . . . but it was seldom she laughed.

My desire for the girl had become heavy and big during the days she had kept out of sight. It was more than the thrust of my loins; for I had known pity for her, and pity breeds passion in men.

One evening after the snow was all gone, I came and sat by her side on a ridge overlooking our camp where she had gone to watch the deer streaming by. I spoke awkwardly of my love. Kala turned her face from me, but one hand crept to my arm and touched the place where I had thrust the knife into my vein. That night, as we all lay together inside the big tent, she came into my arms and we became husband and wife.

Such was my finding of Kala—a finding that brought me the happiest days of my life, for she was a woman of women. Her sewing was gifted by spirits, and her cooking made even Ungyala grow fat. She could hunt nearly as well as a man. And she was avid for love, as one who has once nearly drowned is avid for air. We four lived a good life all that summer and it seemed as if Kala had brought many good things to our land. The deer were never so fat, the muskox never so many, the trout in the rivers never so large. Even our two bitch dogs, which had been fruitless for over two years, gave birth to big litters and raised eleven fine pups that became the best sled dogs I ever owned. So we believed the girl was forgiven . . . that the spirits wished her to suffer no more.

On a day of the following winter, Ungyala and I were sent out of the snowhouse and we sat and shivered in the lee of some rocks until we heard the voice of my mother-by-right singing birth songs to the Whispering Ones who flame in the sky.

After the birth of Itkut, our son, a restlessness seemed to come over us all. Kala yearned to return to the sea. Aputna was feeling her years, and longed once again to hear the voices and see the faces of people she had known long ago. As for me, I was anxious to visit some trader and buy the things Ungyala had told me about; especially guns, for I thought that hunting with spears, bows and arrows did not let me show what a fine hunter I had become. Only Ungyala thought that perhaps we should stay where we were. He remembered too well that he and Aputna had twice had to flee for their lives when the people in the camps where they were living were struck down by the new kind of dying that came from beyond the borders of the Innuit lands. Yet in his heart he too wished to see people again, so we decided to go.

We had two good teams and two sleds. We drove north and then east, making a broad detour around the now empty camps where I had been born. We saw no sign of living men until we finally came to Big River. There we met two families who spent their summers near Eskimo Point and their winters inland on the edge of the plains. We stayed with them for the rest of that winter, hearing much about a world Ungyala and Aputna had almost forgotten and that Kala and I had never known. In the spring, before the ice softened, we followed Big River down to the coast.

So we took up a new way of life. Every autumn we journeyed in a big canoe, with our dogs running free on the shore, up Big River to a lake near its head where the southbound deer crossed a narrows. Here

Ungyala and I speared fat bucks in the water and shot more of them out on the bare, rocky plains with the rifles we had traded for at the coast. By the time the first snows drove the deer out of the land, we would have more than enough meat for the winter, plenty of fat for our lamps, and the best of hides for our clothing and robes.

In the late days of autumn, after the deer had passed and before we began trapping white foxes, there was little to do. Sometimes then I would sit and think and weigh up the worth of my life. It was good, but I understood that its goodness dwelt mainly in Kala. I loved her for the son she had borne, for the clothes that she made me, for the help that she gave me . . . but it went beyond that. I do not know how to explain it, but Kala held me in her soul. The love she gave me passed far beyond respect for a husband and entered that country of pleasure which we of the People do not often know. Such was our life as the child, Itkut, grew with the years.

Now I must tell how it was when we came to the coast. There we met the first white man we had ever seen. It was he who built the wood house at the mouth of Big River. He seemed a good man in some ways, but he was crazy for women. Before he had lived in the country a year, there were few women who had not spent a night in his house, for it was still our law then that a man might not refuse any gift that lay in his giving if another man asked. Kala never went to the house of the white man, though he asked me for her many times. He put shame upon me, for I was forced to refuse.

In the autumn of our fourth year in the new land, we had gone up the river as usual and made our camp at the lake of the Deer Crossing. Ours was the farthest camp from the sea, for we had come from the inland plains and they held no terrors for us. The coast dwellers did not care to go as far as we went. Our tent was pitched within sight of the ford and from the door we could look to see if the deer had arrived.

The time came when the forerunners of the big herd should have appeared, but the crossing remained empty of life. The darkening lichens on the bank were unmarked by the feet of the deer. The dwarf shrubs began to burn red in the first frosts. Ungyala and I walked many miles over the land, climbing the hills and staring out to the north. We saw none of the usual harbingers of the great herds— no ravens floating black in the pale sky, no wolves drifting white on the dark land.

Although we were worried, nothing was said. Kala and Aputna became very busy fishing for trout, suckers and char in the river. They caught little, for the autumn run was nearly over, yet they fished night and day. The dogs began to grow hungry and their howling became so loud we had to move them some miles from the camp in case they frightened the deer. Thinking back to those days I wonder if it was hunger alone that made them so distressed. Maybe they already knew what we would not believe could be true.

The morning came when snow blew in the air . . . only a thin mist of fine snow but enough to tell us that winter had come and it had not brought the deer.

But a few days afterwards the deer came. Ungyala and I went out with light hearts but only a few deer had come to the river. These few were so poor and lacking in fat that we knew they were not the forerunners of the great herds but stragglers that lagged behind, being either too weak or too sick to keep up. We knew then that the deer spirit had led the herds southward by some different path.

The next day there were no deer at the crossing and none to be seen anywhere upon the sweep of the plains, and we had killed barely enough meat to feed ourselves and the dogs for two months.

The real snows came and we began the winter with hearts that were shaken by misgivings. We thought of abandoning our camp and trying to make our way to the coast but we could not do this until enough snow had fallen to make sled travel possible. So we stayed where we were, hoping we would find some of the solitary winter deer that sometimes remain in the land. Ungyala and I roamed with pack dogs over the country for many long miles. A few hares and ptarmigan fell to our guns, but these were no more than food for our hopes.

Before long we ran out of fat, then there was neither light nor heat in the snowhouse. One day Ungyala and I resolved to travel southeast on a journey to some distant islands of little trees where in times past deer used to winter. We took only one small team of dogs, but even these we could not feed and they soon weakened until after a few days they could go no farther. That night we camped in the lee of some cliffs and it was too cold to sleep so we sat and the old man talked of the days of his youth. He was very weak and his voice almost too low to hear. At last he dozed and I covered him with both our robes; but before the dawn he had ceased to breathe, and so I buried my father-by-right in the snow in a grave I cut with my snowknife.

I turned back, but before I reached the snowhouse I heard women's voices singing the song of the dead. Aputna had seen the death of Ungyala in the eye of her mind, and the two women were mourning.

A little time after the death of Ungyala, I wakened one night to the muted whispering of the women. I lay with my face turned to the wall and listened to what Kala was saying to my mother-by-right.

"My mother, the time is not yet come for you to take your old bones to sleep in the snow. Your rest will come after. Now comes a time when I have need of your help."

I knew then that Aputna had decided to take the way of release, and had been held from it by Kala. I did not understand why my wife had restrained her, for it is the right of the old ones that they be the first to die when starvation comes to a camp. But I had small time to wonder, for Kala moved over beside me and spoke softly in my ear, and she told me what I dreaded to hear—that now I must take the few dogs that were left and make my way eastward, down river, until I found a camp that had meat to spare.

I refused, and I called her a fool, for she knew the other camps could be no better off than we were. Kala had always been a woman of sense yet I could not make her see that such a trip would be useless. I knew, and she knew, I could not hope to find help until I reached the coast camps where people depended more on seal meat than on deer, and such a trip, there and back with weak dogs, could not take less than a month. It would be better, I told her, if we killed and ate all the dogs, let my mother-by-right go to her rest, and wait where we were, eking out our lives by fishing for what little could be caught through holes in the ice. Then, if it came to the worst, we three, Kala and Itkut and I, would at least lie down for the last time together.

She would not heed what I said and I heard for the first time the hard edge of anger in her voice.

"You *will* go!" she whispered fiercely. "If you do not, I shall myself put the noose of release on your son when you are gone out of the snowhouse and so save him from the torments that were mine in a time you remember."

And . . . oh, Kipmetna . . . though I knew she was wrong, I could no longer refuse. No, and I did not, although I should have guessed at that which was hidden deep in her thoughts.

At parting next day only the old woman wept. There were no tears from Kala who knew what she knew, and none from young Itkut who was still too young to know what was afoot.

That was a journey! I walked eight days to the nearest camps of the people, for the dogs were too weak to do more than haul the empty sled along at a crawl. In that first camp I found it was as I had feared. Famine had got there before me. Things were nearly as bad all the way down the river. One by one I killed my dogs to keep me and their remaining brothers and sisters alive, and sometimes I shared a little of that lean, bitter meat with people in the camps that I passed.

I was almost in sight of the sea when I came to the camp of my song-cousin, Tanugeak. He and those with him were in good health for they had been living on the meat and the fat of seals Tanugeak had speared far out on the sea ice. They had none too much, though, for they had been helping feed many people who had already fled east from the inland camps. All the same, Tanugeak proved his friendship. He gave me four seals and loaned me five of his own strong dogs, together with fish enough to feed them on the long journey home.

My strength was not much, but I began the up-river journey at once and I sang to the dogs as they ran strongly to the west. I had been away from my camp only two weeks, and now I hoped to return there in eight days at the most. So I sang as the sled ran smoothly over the hard river ice.

Two days up river and a few miles north of my track was a lake and by it two camps where I had stopped overnight on my way to the sea. In those camps I had been given soup made of old bones by people who were almost old bones themselves. Now, with much food on my sled, I did not turn off to give them at least a little of my meat and fat. I told myself I could spare neither the time nor the food if I was to save my own family from death . . . but I knew I did wrong. As my sled slipped into the darkening west I felt a foreboding and I almost turned back. If only I had . . . but such thoughts are useless, and they are a weakness in man; for he does what he does, and he must pay what he pays.

I decided to drive all that night, but when darkness came on it brought a blizzard that rose, full blown, right in my face. The thundering wind from the northwest lashed me with piercing arrows of snow until I could not tell where I was, and the dogs would face it no more. At last I made camp, turning the sled on its side and making a hole in a snowbank nearby for myself. I did not unharness the dogs but picketed them in their traces some way from the sled. Then I crawled into my robes, intending only to doze until the wind dropped. But I was more weary than I knew and I was soon so sound asleep that even the roar of the blizzard faded out of my mind.

All unknowing because of the storm, I had made my camp less than a mile upwind from another camp of the people. The surviving dogs of that camp were roaming about, a famished and half-mad pack. As I slept, they winded my load of seal meat.

I heard nothing until the damage was done. Only when the marauders attacked my own dogs did I awake. In my anguish and rage I flung myself on those beasts with only my small knife as a weapon. The dogs turned upon me and, though I killed some, the smell of fresh blood drove the remainder to fury. They tore the deerskin clothes from my body, savaged one arm until I dropped the knife, and slashed my face until the flesh hung down over my chin. They would have killed me if the fight with my own dogs had not drawn them off, leaving me to crawl back to my hole in the snow.

The morning broke clear and calm, as if no wind had ever blown. I could only manage to stand and shuffle about, and I went to the sled, but the meat was all gone. Nothing was left but some shreds of skin and some bones. Two of my own dogs had been killed and the remainder were hurt.

There was nothing to do. I began to look for my rifle in the debris near the sled but before I could find it I heard dogs howl in the distance and when I looked to the west I saw the domes of three snowhouses below the bank of the river. I turned and shuffled toward them.

I remember but little of the days I spent in that camp because my wounds festered and I was often unconscious. Those people were kind and they fed me with food they could ill spare—though in truth it was partly my food, for it was the meat of the dogs who had eaten the seals. Before I could travel again, the sun had begun to grow warm and to rise higher up in the sky. Yet the warmth of the oncoming spring could not thaw the chill in my heart.

I made a light sled for the two dogs I had left and prepared to depart. Those in the camps tried to keep me with them for they said that by now there would be no life in my snowhouse that stood by the lake of the deer crossing, and I would only die there myself if I returned before spring brought the deer herds back to the land.

But I did not fear death anymore so I set out. Weak as we were, the dogs and I made the journey home in ten days. We had luck, for we found a deer cache that must have been lost by some hunter in the spring of the previous year. It was a foul mess of hair, bones and long-rotted meat, but it gave us the strength to continue.

When we came in sight of the lake my belly grew sick and my legs weakened and I could hardly go on; yet when I neared the camp life pounded back through my veins . . . for the snowhouse still stood and the snow had recently been dug away from the door!

I shouted until my lungs crackled in the bright, cold air and when none answered, I began to run. I reached the passage and scrambled inside.

Abruptly Anoteelik ceased speaking. He sat staring out over the lightening waters of the Bay . . . out toward the islands that were still no more than grey wraiths on the shifting horizon. Tears were running down his disfigured cheeks . . . running like rain. Then with his head bowed forward over his knees, very quietly he finished the tale.

I was greeted by Aputna, my mother-by-right, and by Itkut. The old woman had shrunk to a miserable rag of a thing that should have been gone long ago; but Itkut seemed strong and his body was firm to the touch when I took him up in my arms.

I looked over his shoulder, and asked, "Where is Kala?" though I knew what the answer would be.

Aputna's reply was no louder than the whisper of wind on the hills.

"What was done . . . was done as she wished. As for me, I will not go away from this place, yet I only did what she said must be done . . . and Itkut still lives. . . . Where is Kala? Hold your son close in your arms, love him well for the blood in his veins. Hold him close, oh, my son, for you hold your wife too in your arms."

When the ice left the river, Itkut and I came back down to the coast. Kala was of the Sea People, so I took her bones out to that island which lies far from the shore. While I live I shall take gifts to her spirit each spring . . . in the spring, when the birds make love on the slopes and the does come back to our land, their bellies heavy with fawn.

The Woman and the Wolf

The people built the little snowhouse and departed into the western lands. They went from the place singing laments for the dying, and they left nothing behind them except the old man. They took Arnuk, the dog, that being the old man's wish, for Arnuk was the last gift an old man could make to his son and to his grandson and to his people.

It had been a hard time—those long, hungry months before the spring—and in the camp there had been the cries of children who were too young to know that starvation must be faced in silence. There had been death in the camp, not of men but of those who were of the utmost importance to the continuance of human life. The dogs had died, one by one, and as each was stilled so men's hopes for the future shrank.

Though it had been a harsh time, no word had been spoken against the folly of feeding one old and useless human body. Maktuk, the son, had shared his own meagre rations equally between his aged father and his hungry child who also bore the name that linked the three together. But one dark April day the old man raised himself slowly from the sleeping ledge and gazed for a little while at his grandchild. Then out of the depths of a great love, and a greater courage, old Maktuk spoke:

"I have it in my heart," he said, "that the deer await you at the Western Lakes, but I stay here. You shall take Arnuk with you so that in the years ahead you will remember me."

The old man had his rights, and this was his final one. In the morning the people were gone, and behind young Maktuk's sled the dog Arnuk tugged convulsively at her tether and turned her head backward to stare at a small white mound rising against the snow ridges.

Arnuk had been born two winters earlier, but she was the ninth pup of the litter and so there was little food for her. If the old man had not taken it upon himself to feed and care for her, she would have died before her life truly began. With his help she saw warm days come and tasted the pleasures of long days romping with other young dogs by the side of the great river where the summer camp was pitched. When she grew tired she would come to the skin tent and push against the old man's knees until he opened his eyes and smiled at her.

So she grew through the good times of youth and the people in the camp looked at her with admiration for she became beautiful and of a size and strength surpassing that of any other dog in the camp. Maktuk, the elder, gave her the name she bore, Arnuk—The Woman—for she was wife and daughter to him in the autumn of his years.

Because there can be no death while there is birth, old Maktuk decided in mid-winter that his dog should be mated, although famine had already struck the camp. It was arranged, and so Arnuk bore within her the promise of a strength which would be the people's strength in years to come. When Maktuk, the elder, felt the throb of new life in the womb of The Woman, he was content.

Hunger grew with the passing days. The older dogs died first, then even Arnuk's litter mates lay silent in the snows. But Arnuk's strength was great; and when there was some scrap of bone or skin the people could spare, she received it—for in her womb lay the hopes of years to come.

This was the way things stood when the people turned from the little snowhouse and set their faces to the west, dragging the sleds with their own failing muscles.

The ties that bind man and his dog can be of many strengths, but the ties that bound Arnuk to old Maktuk were beyond human power to sunder. Arnuk went with the people, but resisting stubbornly. On the third night of the journey she gnawed through the rawhide tether and vanished into the swirling ground drift. In the morning Maktuk, the son, held the frayed tether in his hand and his face was shadowed by foreboding. Yet when he spoke to his family it was with these words:

"The Woman has gone to my father and she will be with him when the Snow Walker comes. But my father's spirit will know of our need, and perhaps the day will dawn when he will return The Woman to us."

Arnuk reached the little igloo before daybreak and when the old man opened his eyes to see if it was the Snow Walker, he saw the dog instead. He smiled and laid his bony hand upon her head, and once more he slept.

The Snow Walker was late in coming, but on the third day he came unseen; and when he passed from the place, the bond between man and dog was broken. Yet Arnuk lingered beside her dead for another day, and then it was perhaps the wind that whispered the unspoken order: "Go to the people. Go!"

When she emerged from the snowhouse she found the plains newly scoured by a blizzard. For awhile she stood in the pale winter sun, her lambent coat gleaming against the blue shadows, then she turned her face with its broad ruff and wide-spaced amber eyes toward the west. That way lay her path, and within her the voices of the unborn generations echoed the voice of the wind but with greater urgency. "Go to the places of men," they told her. "Go!"

Head down and great plume held low, she moved westward into the pathless spaces and only once did she pause to turn and stare at her back trail, waiting for some final sign. There was no sign, and at length she turned away.

This was the beginning of her journey. Death had released her from the ties that held her to one man, but she was still bound fast to Man. Through untold generations stretching back through the long dim sweep of time before the Eskimos drifted east across the island chain from Asia, the fate of her kind had been one with that of Man. Arnuk was one with the people and her need of them was as great as their need of her.

She did not halt when darkness swept the bleak plains into obscurity. At midnight she came to the place where she had chewed her way free of young Maktuk's sled. She knew it was the place only by an inner sense, for the snow had levelled all signs and drifted in all trails. Uncertainty began to feed upon her as she circled among the hard drifts, whining miserably. She climbed a rock ridge to test the night air for some sign that men were near. A scent came to her—the odour of an arctic hare that had fled at her approach. But there was no scent of man.

Her whines rose to a crescendo, pleading in the darkness, but there was no answer except the rising mutter of the wind. Unable to endure the weight of her hunger and loneliness, she curled up in the shelter of a drift and lost herself in dreams.

So the dog slept in the heart of the great plains. But even as she dozed restlessly, a profound change was taking place in the secret places of her body. She lay with her nose outstretched on her broad forepaws and her muscles twitched with erratic impulses. Saliva flowed in her mouth and had the taste of blood. In her mind's eye she laid her stride to that of the swift deer, and her teeth met in the living flesh and she knew the ecstasy of the hunter.

From out of time the ageless instincts which lie in all living cells were being revitalized so that the dog, and the new life within her, would not perish. When Arnuk raised her head to the dawn light, the thing was done, the change complete.

The dawn was clear, and Arnuk, her perceptions newly honed, tested the wind. When she found the warm aroma of living flesh she went to seek it out.

A Snowy Owl, dead white and shadowless in the pre-dawn, had swept across the plains with great eyes staring. The owl had seen and fallen on a hare so swiftly that the beast had known nothing until the inch-long talons took life from him. For a little time the great bird chose to savour its hunger; and while it sat complacently crouched above the hare, it did not see the flow of motion behind a nearby drift.

Arnuk was a weasel easing up on a lemming, a fox drifting toward a ptarmigan. Skills she had never fully known had come alive within her. She inched forward soundlessly over the hard snows. When she was still a few yards from the owl, it raised its head and the yellow eyes stared with expressionless intensity full into Arnuk's face. Arnuk was the stillness of death, yet every muscle vibrated. When the owl turned back to its prey, Arnuk leapt. The owl saw the beginning of the leap and threw itself backward into its own element with a smooth thrust of mighty wings. Those wings were a fraction slow and the hurtling form of the dog, leaping six feet into the air, struck flesh beneath the feathers.

Arnuk slept afterwards while white feathers blew into the distance and tufts of white fur moved like furtive living things in the grip of the wind. When she woke again the age-old voices within her had quieted. Once more she was man's beast, and so she set out again into the west, unconscious yet directly driven.

The people whom she sought were wanderers on the face of a plain so vast that it seemed limitless. The dog could not envisage the odds against her finding them, but in her memory was the image of the summer camp by the wide river where she had spent her youth. She set her mind upon that distant place.

The days passed and the sun stood a little higher in the sky after each one faded. Time passed under the dog's feet until the explosion of spring overwhelmed the tundra. The snows melted and the rivers awoke and thundered seaward. Flights of ravens hung like eddies of burned leaves in a white and glaring sky, and on the thawing ponds the first ducks mingled with raucous flocks of gulls.

Life quickened in the deep moss where the lemmings tunnelled and on the stony ridges where cock ptarmigan postured before their mates. It was in all living things and in all places, and it was within the womb of the dog. Her journey had been long and her broad paws were crusted with the dried blood of many stone cuts. Her coat was matted and lustreless under the spring suns. Still she drew upon her indomitable will and went forward into the western plains.

Gaunt and hot eyed she brought her quest to an end on a day in June. Breasting a long ridge she saw before her the glittering light of sun on roaring water and she recognized the river.

Whining with excitement she ran clumsily down the slope, for her body had grown awkward in these last days. Soon she was among the rings of weathered boulders where, in other summers, men's tents had stood.

No tents stood there now. There were no living men to welcome the return of the lost one. Only the motionless piles of rocks on nearby ridges, that are called *Inukok*, Men of Stone, were there to welcome Arnuk. She understood that the place was abandoned yet for a time she refused to believe it. She ran from old tent ring to old meat cache, sniffing each with a despairing hope, and finding nothing to give her heart. It was dusk before she curled herself in a hollow beside the place where Maktuk, the elder, had once held her at his knees, and gave herself up to her great weariness.

Yet the place was not as deserted as it looked. While Arnuk was making her fruitless search she was too preoccupied to realize that she was being watched. If she had glanced along the river bank she might have seen a lithe shape that followed her every move with eyes that held in them a hunger not born of the belly. She would have seen and recognized a wolf, and her hackles would have risen and her teeth been bared. For the dogs of men and the dogs of the wilderness walk apart, theirs being the hostility of brothers who deny their common blood.

The wolf was young. Born the preceding season, he had stayed with his family until, in the early spring of this year, the urge to wander had come over him and he had forsaken his clan's territory. Many adventures had befallen him and he had learned, at the cost of torn flanks and bleeding shoulders, that each wolf family guards its own land and there is no welcome for a stranger. His tentative approaches had been met with bared teeth in the lands of three wolf clans before he came to the river and found a place where no wolves were.

It was a good place. Not far from the empty Innuit camp the river flared over a shallow stretch of jagged boulders to lose itself in the beginning of an immense lake, and here for centuries the caribou had forded the shallows during their migrations. Two or three times a year they crossed the river in untold thousands, and not all escaped the river's surge. Drowned bodies of dead deer lay among the rocks at the river mouth, giving food to many foxes, ravens and white gulls. The wolves of the country did not visit the place because it belonged to man, and that which man claims to himself is abhorrent to the great wild dogs.

Knowing nothing of this tabu, the young male wolf, the wanderer, had taken up his home by the river; and here he nursed his loneliness, for even more than dogs, wolves are social beings.

When the young wolf saw and smelled Arnuk, he was filled with conflicting emotions. He had seen no dog before but he sensed that the golden-coated

111

beast below him was somehow of his blood. The smell was strange, and yet it was familiar. The shape and colour were strange, and yet they roused in him a warmth of memory and desire. But he had been rebuffed so many times that he was cautious now.

When Arnuk woke she did not at first see the stranger, but her nostrils told her of the nearness of deer meat. Her hunger was overpowering. She leapt to her feet and flung herself upon a ragged haunch of caribou that had been dragged to within a few yards of her sleeping place. Only when she had satisfied her first hunger did she glance up . . . to meet the still gaze of the young wolf.

He sat motionless a hundred feet from her and did not even twitch an ear as Arnuk's hackles lifted and the threat took form deep in her throat. He remained sitting quietly but tense to spring away, and after a long minute Arnuk again dropped her head to the meat.

This was the way of their first meeting, and this is what came of it.

Arnuk could no longer resist the insistent demands of her heavy body. Once again the hidden force within her took command. Ignoring the young wolf, who still cautiously kept his distance, Arnuk made a tour of the familiar ground beside the river. She carefully examined the carcasses of five drowned deer and chased away the screaming gulls and guttural ravens, for this meat was hers now by right of greater strength. Then, satisfied with the abundant food supply, she left the river and trotted inland to where a rock outcrop had opened its flanks to form a shallow cave. Here, as a pup, Arnuk had played with the other dogs of the camp. Now she examined the cave with more serious intent. The place was dry and protected from the winds. There was only one thing wrong, and that was the smell. The rock cleft was pervaded with a potent and unpleasant stench that caused Arnuk to draw back her lips in anger and distaste—a wolverine had bedded in the cave during the winter months.

Arnuk's nose told her that the wolverine had been gone for several weeks, and there seemed little likelihood that he would return until the winter gales again forced him to seek shelter. She scratched earth and sand over the unclean floor, then set about dragging moss into the deepest recess. Here she hid herself and made surrender to her hour.

Arnuk's pups were born on a morning when the cries of the white geese were loud in the spring air. It was the time of birth, and the seven squirming things that lay warm against the dog's fur were not alone in their first day of life. On the sand ridges beyond the river, female ground squirrels suckled naked motes of flesh; and in a den by a ridge a mile distant, an arctic fox thrust his alert face above the ground while the feeble whimpers of the pups his mate was nursing warned him of the tasks ahead. All living things in the land by the river moved to the rhythm of the demands of life newborn or soon to be born. All things moved to this rhythm except the outcast wolf.

During the time Arnuk remained hidden, the young wolf underwent a torment that gave him no peace. Restless and yearning for things he had never known, he haunted the vicinity of the cave. He did not dare go too close, but each day he carried a piece of deer meat to within a few yards of the cave mouth and then drew back to wait hopefully for his gift to be accepted.

On the third day, as he lay near the cave snapping at the flies which hung in a cloud about his head, his keen ears felt the faintest tremors of a new

113

sound. He was on his feet instantly, head thrust out and body tense with attention. It came again, so faint it was felt rather than heard—a tiny whimper that called to him across the ages and across all barriers. He shook himself abruptly and with one quick, proprietary glance at the cave mouth, he trotted out across the plain—no longer a solitary outcast but a male beginning the evening hunt that would feed his mate and pups. So, simply and out of his deep need, the young wolf filled the void that had surrounded him through the torturing weeks of spring.

Arnuk did not so easily accept the wolf in his newly assumed role. For several days she kept him at a distance with bared teeth, although she ate the food he left at the cave mouth. But before a week was out she had come to expect the fresh meat—the tender ground squirrels, arctic hares and plump ptarmigan. From this acceptance it was not a very long step to complete acceptance of the wolf himself.

Arnuk sealed the compact with him during the second week after the pups were born, when, coming to the den mouth one morning, she found part of a freshly killed caribou fawn lying ready for her, and the sleeping form of the young wolf only a few feet away.

The wolf had made a long, hard hunt that night, covering most of the hundred square miles of territory he had staked out for his adopted family. Exhausted by his efforts, he had not bothered to retire the usual discreet distance from the den.

For a long minute Arnuk stared at the sleeping wolf and then she began to stalk him. There was no menace in her attitude and when she reached the wolf's side her great plumed tail went up into its husky curl and her lips lifted as if in laughter.

The wolf woke, raised his head, saw her standing

114

over him and knew that here at last was the end to loneliness. The morning light blazed over the den ridge as the two stood shoulder to shoulder looking out over the awakening plains.

Life was good by the banks of the river during the days that followed. There was no emptiness now in Arnuk's heart. And for the wolf there was the swelling pride with which he lay in the sun outside the den while the pups tussled with his fur and chewed at his feet.

Time passed until the pups were in their seventh week. Midsummer had come to the barrens and the herds of deer were drifting southward again. The crossing place was once more thronged and calves grunted beside their ragged mothers while old bucks, their velvet-covered antlers reaching to the skies, moved aloofly in the van.

One evening a hunger for the chase came over Arnuk, and in the secret ways men know nothing of, she made her desire known to the wolf. When the late summer dusk fell, Arnuk went out alone into the darkening plains, secure in the knowledge that the wolf would steadfastly guard the pups until she returned.

She did not intend a long absence, but several miles from the river she came on a band of young buck deer. They were fine beasts, and fat, which at this time of the year was unusual. Arnuk was tired of lean meat and she circled the resting herd, filled with an ardent appetite.

A change of the uncertain breeze betrayed her and the startled deer sprang to their feet and fled. Arnuk was hungry and the night was a hunter's night. She took up the long chase.

The hours drove the brief darkness from the land and when the early winds of dawn rose in the north the young wolf roused himself from his vigil at the

115

cave mouth. An ill-defined uneasiness made him turn to the den and thrust his head and shoulders into the entrance. All was well, and the pups were rolled together in a compact ball, jerking their sturdy legs in sleep. Yet the prickle of anxiety persisted in the wolf's mind and he turned toward the river where the grey light picked out the long rolls of distant ridges.

Perhaps he was worried by Arnuk's long absence; or perhaps he had been disturbed by senses unknown to man. He trotted away from the den sniffing at the cold trail of the dog, hoping to see her approaching across the lightening plains.

He had gone no more than a quarter of a mile when the vague sense of something amiss took concrete form. A vagrant eddy brought the north breeze to his nostrils and instantly he knew what had disturbed him when he woke. He sprinted back toward the cave with startling speed.

As he breasted the slope beside the den the stink of wolverine filled his nostrils and he was transformed by an elemental fury. He came down the slope in half a dozen gigantic leaps, ears flat to his skull and his throat rumbling with incoherent rage.

The wolverine which had wintered in the cave where Arnuk's pups now whimpered in their sleep was a sixty-pound male, a little past his prime, and more than a little short of temper. That spring he had methodically searched for a mate across hundreds of miles of the surrounding country and had found none. During the night of Arnuk's hunt he had returned to the ford by the river where he expected to find a good store of drowned deer. Instead he had found nothing but clean bones and the evidence that a wolf and a dog had pre-empted what he considered to be his private larder. His mood grew worse, and when

116

his wrinkling nostrils caught the faintest trace of pup smell from the direction of the old winter lair, he did not hesitate. His belly rumbling with hunger he turned from the river in the grey dawn light and circled upwind until he found a rock outcrop that gave him cover and from which he could observe the den. Here he waited until he saw the young wolf trot away from the den mouth toward the inland plains.

Cautiously the wolverine moved in upon the den, pausing to reassure himself that the pups were undefended. His massive body hugged the rough ground as he drew closer and now, certain of success, he could foretaste the pleasure of the killing and the salt warmth of blood.

There was blood enough for him to taste that dawn.

The young wolf's furious rush was so swift that the wolverine had only time to slew about and take the weight of the attack upon his side. It was enough to save him for the moment. Although the wolf's teeth sank into the tough skin, they missed their intended hold upon the throat, meeting instead in the muscles of the wolverine's shoulder. On any lesser beast it would have been a good hold, but on this beast it was not good enough. Aflame with an incandescent anger, he swung the wolf clean off its feet as he whirled in a savage counter-thrust.

Had the wolf been older and more experienced he might have released his grip and sidestepped that lunge, but he was young and blinded by the allegiance he had so freely given to the pups he had not sired. He held his grip and did not slacken it even when the wolverine's teeth and claws raked deep into his flank.

They fought in silence. On the eastern rim of the horizon the red sun seemed pallid beside the glare of

117

blood upon the rocks. Drawn to the cave mouth by the first onslaught, the pups watched for an instant and then, terrified by the fury of the struggle, retreated to crouch trembling in the dark earth. Only the gulls witnessed the duel's end.

The gulls warned Arnuk. As she trotted wearily homeward in the warmth of the morning, she saw them circling and heard their strident screams. They eddied ominously above the rocks where the den lay and, weary as she was, anxiety gave her new strength and she came on at a gallop. And so she found them. The wolverine had dragged himself toward the river before he bled to death. But the wolf, his belly ripened raggedly so that his entrails sprawled around him, lay stiffening beside the entrance to the cave.

The bodies still lay where they had died when, a few days later, the voices of men echoed once more along the shores of the river, and young Maktuk bent down to the dark opening and gently thrust his hand under the timid pups while Arnuk, half wild with old emotions, stood trembling by his side. Maktuk was a man who could read much that is never written and he understood all there was to know of what had taken place beneath those shattered rocks.

On an evening in late summer he took his son to the bank of the river and placed the boy's hand on the head of the saffron-coated dog.

"Maktuk, my son, in a little time you also shall be a man and a hunter, and the wide plains will know your name. In those days to come you will have certain friends to help you in the hunt, and of these the foremost you shall always call *Arnuk;* and then my father will know that we received his gift and he will be at ease. And in those times to come, all beasts shall fall to your spear and bow, save one alone. Never shall your hand be raised against the white one—against *Amow*, the wolf—and so shall our people pay their debt to him."

The Snow Walker

I am Ootek, and my people are the people of the River of Men. Once they were many and the land was good to them, but now it is my time and we have almost forgotten how it was in the old days when the deer flooded the tundra and gave us life. Hunger comes often now, and the deer but seldom. No one now lives by the big lakes to the north although when my father was young the tents of the people stood everywhere along those shores. I have travelled down the River to the big lakes but when I reached them I turned back from an empty land.

Only the spirits who remain in those places remember the times when a man might stand on a hill as the deer passed by and though he looked to the east or the west, the south or the north, he would see only their brown backs and hear only the clicking of antlers and the grumbling of their full bellies.

The great herds have gone . . . and so we who

lived by the deer must follow the Snow Walker even as my father followed him in the spring of the year.

After the ice had grown thick on the lakes last winter there came a time of storms and for many days we stayed in our igloos. The children grew quiet and did not play and the old people sometimes looked toward the door tunnels with shadowed eyes. The snows mounted over the top of the igloos until we could not even venture out to look for willow twigs to burn. The igloos were cold and dark for we had long since eaten the deer fat that should have burned in the lamps. So little food remained to us from the few southbound deer we had been able to kill in the autumn that the dogs were beginning to starve, and we ourselves were not much better off.

One day Belikari, who was my closest neighbour among the seven families living in the camp, came to tell me that a mad fox had run into the tunnel of his snowhouse where his dogs lay and had bitten three of them before it was killed by the rest. Those three dogs died with foam at their lips, and they were only three of many. This was another evil because when the foxes went mad their pelts became worthless and so, even if the storms had allowed us to travel, it would have been no use visiting the traps.

After a long time the blizzards ended and the weather grew calm and cold. All the people had survived though some of the old ones could hardly stir from the sleeping ledges. We younger men took the few remaining dogs and went searching for meat we had cached on the Flat Country. We found only a little because most of the caches were buried under hard drifts that had mounted so high they had covered the markers.

The women and children helped to keep famine

at bay by digging under the drifts near the igloos for fish bones and scraps of old hides with which to make soup. By such means we hoped to cling to our lives until the warm winds and the lengthening days might bring the deer back to our country from the forested lands in the south.

But long after the time when the ice should have started to rot, it still lay heavy and hard on the rivers and lakes, and the days seemed to grow colder again until we wondered if winter would ever come to an end. We ate all the food we had, and the deer did not come. We waited . . . for there was nothing else we could do. We ate the last of our dogs, and still the deer did not come.

One day the men gathered in Owliktuk's snowhouse. His wife, Kunee, sat on the ledge with her child in her arms, and the child was dead. We knew it could not be very long before many of the women were nursing such sorrow. My cousin, Ohoto, put some thoughts into words.

"Perhaps people should go away from this place now. Perhaps they might go south to the place where the white man has come to live. It might happen that he would have food he would give us."

The white man had only recently come to live on the edge of our country, to trade with us for foxes. It was a long way to his place and only Ohoto had been there before. Since we had no dogs, we knew we would have to carry everything on our backs, and the children and old people would not be able to ride on the sleds as they should. We knew some of them would not see the white man's place . . . but the child of Owliktuk and Kunee was dead. We decided to go.

The women rolled up a few skins to use for tent shelters and sleeping robes; the children carried whatever they could, and we men slung our packs on our shoulders and we left our camp by the River and set out into the south.

Soon after we started, the sun turned warm and for five days we walked up to our knees in melting snow. My wife's mother had lost count of the years she had lived, yet she walked with the rest and still helped to pitch camp at the end of each day. But on the fifth night she did not offer to help. She sat by herself with her back to a rock and spoke to none except Ilupalee, my daughter. She called the child to her.

From a distance I watched and listened as the old woman put her bony hands on my daughter's head. I heard her softly singing her spirit song to the child, the secret song she had received from her mother's mother and with which she could summon her helping spirit. Then I knew she had made up her mind what she must do.

It was her choice, and my wife and I could say nothing about it, not even to tell her of the sorrow we felt. During the night, she went from the camp. None saw her go. We did not speak her name after that for one may not use the name of a person who has gone out on the land to seek the Snow Walker until the name and the spirit it bears can be given again to a newly born child.

The next day we reached the Little Stick country which borders the forests. Here there was plenty of wood so we could at least have fires where we could warm ourselves. Toward evening we overtook Ohoto's family squatted beside a fire, melting water to drink since there was no food. Ohoto told me his daughter had fallen and could not rise again so they had to make camp. When the rest of the people came up, it was clear that many, both young and old, could not go on; and Ohoto thought we were still two or three days distant from the home of the white man.

I had been carrying Ilupalee on my shoulders most of the day and was so tired I could not think. I lay down by the fire and shut my eyes. Ilupalee lay beside me and whispered in my ear:

"A white hare is sitting behind the little trees over there."

I thought this was only a dream born out of hunger so I did not open my eyes. But she whispered again:

"It is a big, fat hare. She Who Walked said it was there."

This time I opened my eyes and got to my knees. I looked where she pointed and could see nothing except a patch of dwarf spruce. All the same I unslung the rifle from my pack and walked toward the trees.

Indeed it was there!

But one hare does not provide more than a mouthful of food for twenty-five people so we had to think carefully what should be done. It was decided that the three strongest men—Alekahaw, Ohoto and I—would eat the hare and thereby gain strength to go on to the white man's place. My wife built a fire apart from the camp so the others would not have to endure the smell of meat cooking. She boiled the hare and we three men shared it; but we left the guts, bones, skin and the head to make soup for the children.

We walked away from the camp along a frozen stream so we would not have to wade through the soft snow. My skin boots were thin and torn and my feet were soon numb because at each step we broke through the thin crust above the thaw water. I did not mind because my stomach was warm.

It was growing dark on the second day when we came to a clearing in a spruce woods on the shore of a lake where the white man had his house. His dogs heard us and howled and when we came near he opened the door and waited with the bright light of a lamp shining behind him. We stopped and stood where we were because he was a stranger, and a white man, and we had met very few white men. He spoke to us, but not in our language, so we could not reply. When he spoke again, very loudly, and still we did not reply, he went back into his house.

It grew cold as the darkness settled around us, and our wet boots became stiff as they froze. I thought of Ilupalee and wanted very much to do something, but did not know what we should do.

After a long time the door opened again and the white man came out. He was wiping his beard. We smelled hot fat from his house but he shut the door behind him and motioned us to follow him to another small cabin.

He unlocked the door and we went in. He lit a lamp and hung it on a rafter so we could see that the walls were piled high with boxes, but we looked hardest at the many bags of flour stacked in front of a table. We started to smile for we believed the white man understood our needs and would help us. We stood under the lamp watching the flame reflect light from the beads of cold fat still clinging to the white man's beard, and we gave ourselves up to the joy growing within us.

The white man opened a drawer in the table and took out a handful of small sticks of the kind used to show how much a trapper can have in exchange for the fox pelts he brings. Holding these sticks in his hand he spoke sharply in his own tongue. When we did not reply he went to a wall of the cabin, took down a fox pelt and laid it before us; then he pointed to the carrying bags which were slung on our shoulders.

The joy went out of us then. I made signs to show we had no fox pelts to trade, and Alekahaw opened his bag to show how empty it was. The white man's eyes were of a strange green colour and I could not look into them. I looked at his forehead instead while I waited for whatever must happen. Slowly his face grew red with anger, then he threw the sticks back in the drawer and began to shout at us.

Anger is something we fear since an angry man may do foolish and dangerous things. When I saw the anger in this man's face. I backed to the door. I wanted to go from that place but Alekahaw was braver than me. He stood where he was and tried to explain to the white man how it was at the camp where the rest of the people were starving. He pulled up his *holiktu* so the man could see for himself how Alekahaw's ribs stuck out from his body. Alekahaw touched his own face to show how tightly the skin was stretched over the bones.

The white man shrugged his shoulders. Perhaps he did not understand. He began turning down the flame in the lamp and we knew he would soon go back to his house, then the door would be shut against the needs of the people. Quickly Ohoto pulled two boxes of shells out of his bag. These were the last bullets he had and he had been saving them against the time when the deer would return. Now he put them on the table and pointed to the flour.

The white man shook his head. He was still angry. He picked up the lamp and started to go to the door. Alekahaw and Ohoto stepped out of his way, but something happened inside me and although I was frightened I would not let him pass.

He kept his eyes on me but he stretched out one hand behind him until it came to rest on a rifle hung on the wall. I could not make way for him then because I was afraid to move while he had his hand on that gun.

So we all stood still for a while. At last he picked up a small sack of flour and threw it over the table to fall at Ohoto's feet. Then he took the rifle, shoved me aside with the barrel, pushed the door open and told us to leave. We went outside and watched as he locked the door. We watched as he went back into his house.

A little while later we saw him looking out of his window. He still had the rifle in his hand so we knew there was no use remaining. We walked away into the darkness.

Day was breaking when we got back to the camp. Those who were still able to stand gathered in front of Owliktuk's tent and we told what we had to tell. We showed them the sack of flour which was so small a child could easily lift it.

Owliktuk spoke against us, blaming us because we had not taken the food that was needed. He said we could have repaid the white man next winter when the foxes were again good. But if we had tried to take food from the white man there would have been killing. Perhaps Owliktuk only spoke as he did because his second child was now going from him. The rest of the people said nothing but returned to their families with the small portions of flour which were their shares.

I carried my father's share to his tent. Although he had once been the best hunter among us and only the previous year had fathered a child on his third wife, he had aged very much during the winter and his legs had weakened until he could barely walk. When I told him what had happened and gave him the flour for himself, my stepmother and the small child, he smiled and said, "One has a son who knows what may be done and what may not be done. One is glad no blood was shed. It may be that things will get better."

It did not seem he was right about that. We had made the journey to the white man's place and it had come to so little. Now we were too weak to go back to our own land. And on the second day after we three men returned to the camp, the Snow Walker came to the children Aljut and Uktilohik. There was no mourning for them because those who still lived had no sorrow to spend on the dead.

Each day thereafter the sun shone more brightly. Spring was upon us and still the deer had not returned. One day I tried to visit my father to see how it was with him but I was unable to walk that short distance. I crawled back into my own tent where my wife sat rocking herself with her eyes closed and her mouth wide and gasping. Beside her my daughter sometimes wailed in the thin, dry voice of an old woman. I lay down on some brush inside the flap and together we waited.

Perhaps it was the next day when I awakened to hear someone shout. The shout came again and the voice seemed familiar and the words set my heart racing.

"Here is a deer!"

I caught my rifle by the muzzle and crawled into the morning sunlight. At first I was blinded but after a moment I saw a fine buck standing a little way off with his head high, watching the camp.

I raised my rifle with hands that could not seem to hold it. The sights wavered and the deer seemed to slide up and down the barrel. Clutching it tight, I took aim and fired. The buck flung up his forefeet and leapt toward the sheltering trees. I fired again and again until the rifle was empty but the shots all went wide. I could see them kicking up little spouts of snow but I could not hear the hard thud that tells a hunter when he has hit.

The deer ran away . . . but just when it was about to disappear in the trees it stumbled and fell. With all my strength I willed it not to get up. The deer's spirit struggled with mine until slowly the buck sank on his side.

Some of the people had come out into the sunlight and with weak voices were asking each other who had been shooting.

"Get out your knives!" I cried as loud as I could. "One has killed a fat deer!"

At my words even those who could not walk found enough strength. People wept as they stumbled and staggered toward the deer carcass. The first ones to reach it clung to it like flies, sucking the blood that still bubbled out of its wound. They moved away after a while to make room for others, sobbing with pain and holding their hands to their bellies.

The women sliced into the carcass with their round knives and tore out the entrails, snatching at the little scraps of white fat that clung to the guts. The men cut off the legs at the lower joints and cracked the bones to get at the marrow. In only a short time the buck was changed into a pile of bones, steaming meat and red snow.

It grew warm under the sun and some people began returning to the shelters with meat for those who were too weak to move. Then I remembered that I had seen no one from the tent of my father, so I made my way there dragging part of a forequarter. The flap was down over the door but I pushed it aside and crawled in. My stepmother was lying under a piece of hairless old hide and she was holding her child against her dry dugs. Although they scarcely breathed they were both still alive. But of my father there was no sign.

I cut off a piece of meat, chewed it soft then pushed it into my stepmother's mouth and rubbed her neck till she swallowed. Then I took my little stepbrother to Ohoto's shelter, which was not far away, and Ohoto's wife made blood soup and fed the child with it while I went back to my father's place and chewed more meat for my stepmother. Before I left her, she was able to eat by herself but she could not yet talk so I did not know where my father had gone.

When I returned to my own place, I found my wife had roasted some ribs and boiled the deer's tongue. Ilupalee lay wrapped in a fresh piece of deerskin and it was good to hear her whimper with the pain of a full belly. That whole night we passed in eating and by the next day nothing of the buck remained for the ravens and foxes. The bones had been crushed and boiled for their fat, the skull had been opened and cleaned, and even the hooves had been made into soup. The strength of the buck had passed into the people and we were ready to return to our country.

Next day when I went to my father's tent my stepmother was able to stand. I told her that she and the child would now come and live in my tent, then I said, "One looks about but does not see one's father."

"*Eeee*," she replied. "He would not eat the flour you brought. He gave it to me and the child. Afterwards he went on the land to meet the Snow Walker."

A little while later I told Ohoto about the voice I had heard. No one else had heard it and none of the people in the camp except me had known there was a deer nearby. Together Ohoto and I followed the marks where my father had stumbled down to the

130

river, then crawled north on the ice. His tracks disappeared at a bend where the current had opened a hole, but close by we found the tracks of a deer. We followed the tracks until they circled back to the camp and came to an end at the place where I had killed the big buck. Neither Ohoto nor I said anything but we both knew whose voice I had heard.

In the autumn my wife will give birth to another child, and then the name of him who went to meet the Snow Walker that we might continue to live will surely be spoken again by the River of Men.

Walk Well, My Brother

When Charlie Lavery first went north just after the war, he was twenty-six years old and case hardened by nearly a hundred bombing missions over Europe. He was very much of the new elite who believed that any challenge, whether by man or nature, could be dealt with by good machines in the hands of skilled men. During the following five years, flying charter jobs in almost every part of the arctic from Hudson Bay to the Alaska border, he had found no reason to alter this belief. But though his familiarity with arctic skies and his ability to drive trackless lines across them had become considerable, he remained a stranger to the land below. The monochromatic wilderness of rock and tundra, snow and ice, existed outside his experience and comprehension, as did the native people whose world this was.

One mid-August day in 1951 he was piloting a

war-surplus Anson above the drowned tundra plains south of Queen Maud Gulf, homeward bound to his base at Yellowknife after a flight almost to the limit of the aircraft's range. The twin engines thundered steadily and his alert ears caught no hint of warning from them. When the machine betrayed his trust, it did so with shattering abruptness. Before he could touch the throttles, the starboard engine was dead and the port one coughing in staccato bursts. Then came silence—replaced almost instantly by a rising scream of wind as the plane nosed steeply downward the shining circlet of a pond.

It was too small a pond and the plane had too little altitude. As Lavery frantically pumped the flap hydraulics, the floats smashed into the rippled water. The Anson careened wickedly for a few yards and came to a crunching stop against the frost-shattered rocks along the shore.

Lavery barely glanced at his woman passenger, who had been thrown into a corner of the cabin by the impact. He scrambled past her, flung open the door and jumped down to find himself standing knee deep in frigid water. Both floats had been so badly holed that they had filled and now rested on the rocky bottom.

The woman crawled to the door and Lavery looked up into an oval, warmly tinted face framed in long black hair. He groped for the few Eskimo words he knew:

"*Tingmeak . . . tokoiyo . . .* smashed to hell! No fly! Understand?"

As she stared back uncomprehending, a spasm of anger shook him. What a fool he'd been to take her aboard at all . . . now she was a bloody albatross around his neck.

Four hours earlier he had landed in a bay on the Gulf coast to set out a cache of aviation gas for a prospecting company. No white men lived in that part of the world and Lavery had considered it a lucky accident to find an Eskimo tent pitched there. The two men who had run out to watch him land had been a godsend, helping to unload the drums, float them to tideline and roll them up the beach well above the storm line.

He had given each of them a handful of chocolate bars in payment for their work and had been about to head back for Yellowknife when the younger Eskimo touched his arm and pointed to the tent. Lavery had no desire to visit that squat skin cone hugging the rocks a hundred yards away and it was not the Eskimo's gentle persistence that prevailed on him—it was the thought that these Huskies might have a few white fox pelts to trade.

There were no fox pelts in the tent. Instead there was a woman lying on some caribou hides. *Nuliak*— wife—was the only word Lavery could understand of the Eskimo's urgent attempt at explanation.

The tent stank of seal oil and it was with revulsion that Lavery looked more closely at the woman. She was young and not bad looking—for a Husky—but her cheeks were flushed a sullen red by fever and a trickle of blood had dried at the corner of her mouth. Her dark eyes were fixed upon him with grave intensity. He shook his head and turned away.

T.B. . . . sooner or later all the Huskies got it . . . bound to the filthy way they lived. It would be no kindness to fly her out to the little hospital at Yellowknife already stuffed with dying Indians. She'd be better off to die at home. . . .

Lavery was halfway back to the Anson before the younger Eskimo caught up with him. In his hands he held two walrus tusks, and the pilot saw they were of exceptional quality.

Ah, what the hell . . . no skin off my ass. I'm deadheading anyhow. . . .

"*Eeema*. Okay, I'll take your *nuliak*. But make it snappy. *Dwoee, dwoee!*"

While Lavery fired up the engines, the men carried the woman, wrapped in caribou-skin robes, and placed her in the cabin. The younger Eskimo pointed at her, shouting her name: Konala. Lavery nodded and waved them away. As he pulled clear of the beach he caught a glimpse of them standing in the slipstream, as immobile as rocks. Then the plane was airborne, swinging around on course for the long haul home.

Barely two hours later he again looked into the eyes of the woman called Konala . . . wishing he had never seen or heard of her.

She smiled tentatively but Lavery ignored her and pushed past into the cabin to begin sorting through the oddments which had accumulated during his years of arctic flying. He found a rusty .22 rifle and half a box of shells, a torn sleeping bag, an axe and four cans of pork and beans. This, together with a small box of matches and a pocket knife in his stylish cotton flying jacket, comprised a survival outfit whose poverty testified to his contempt for the world that normally lay far below his aircraft.

Shoving the gear into a packsack he waded ashore. Slowly Konala followed, carrying her caribou robes and a large sealskin pouch. With mounting irritation Lavery saw that she was able to move without much difficulty. Swinging the lead to get a free plane ride, he thought. He turned on her.

"The party's over, lady! Your smart-assed boy

friend's got you into a proper mess—him and his god-damn walrus tusks!"

The words meant nothing to Konala but the tone was clear enough. She walked a few yards off, opened her pouch, took out a fishing line and began carefully unwinding it. Lavery turned his back on her and made his way to a ledge of rock where he sat down to consider the situation.

A thin tongue of fear was flickering in the back of his mind. Just what the hell *was* he going to do? The proper drill would be to stick with the Anson and wait until a search plane found him . . . except he hadn't kept to his flight plan. He had said he intended to fly west down the coast to Bathurst before angling southwest to Yellowknife . . . instead he'd flown a direct course from the cache, to save an hour's fuel. Not so bright maybe, considering his radio was out of kilter. There wasn't a chance in a million they'd look for him this far off-course. Come to that, he didn't even know exactly where he was . . . fifty miles or so north of the Back River lakes would be a good guess. There were so damn few landmarks in this godfor-saken country. . . . Well, so he wasn't going to be picked up . . . that left Shanks' mare, as the Limeys would say . . . but which way to go?

He spread out a tattered aeronautical chart on the knees of his neat cotton pants. Yellowknife, four hundred miles to the southwest, was out of the ques-tion. . . . The arctic coast couldn't be more than a hundred and fifty miles away but there was nobody there except a scattering of Huskies. . . . How about Baker Lake? He scaled off the airline distance with thumb and forefinger, ignoring the innumerable lakes and rivers across the route. About two hundred miles. He was pretty fit . . . should be able to manage twenty miles a day . . . ten days, and presto.

136

Movement caught his eye and he looked up. Konala, a child-like figure in her bulky deerskin clothes, had waded out to stand on the submerged tail of a float. Bent almost double, she was swinging a length of line around her head. She let the weighted hook fly so that it sailed through the air to strike the surface a hundred feet from shore.

Well, there was no way she could walk to Baker. She'd have to stay put until he could bring help. His anger surged up again. . . . Fishing, for God's sake! What in Jesus' sweet name did she think she was going to catch in that lousy little pond?

He began to check his gear. Lord, no *compass* . . . and the sun was no use this time of year. He'd never bothered to buy one of the pocket kind . . . no need for it . . . but there was a magnetic compass in the instrument panel of the old crate. . . .

Lavery hurried back to the Anson, found some tools and went to work. He was too preoccupied to notice Konala haul in her line and deftly slip a fine char off the hook. He did not see her take her curved woman's knife and slice two thick fillets from the fish. The first he knew of her success was when she appeared at the open cabin door. She was so small that her head barely reached the opening. With one hand she held a fillet up to him while with the other she pushed raw pink flesh into her mouth, pantomiming to show him how good it was.

"Jesus, no!" He was revolted and waved her away. "Eat it yourself . . . you animal!"

Obediently Konala disappeared from the doorway. Making her way ashore she scraped together a pile of dry lichens then struck a light with flint and steel. The moss smoked and began to glow. She covered it with dwarf willow twigs, then spread pieces of the fish on two flat rocks angled toward the rising flames. When Lavery descended from the plane with the compass in his hand his appetite woke with a rush at the sight and smell of roasting fish. But he did not go near the fire. Instead he retreated to the rocks where he had left his gear and dug out a can of beans. He gashed his thumb trying to open the can with his pocket knife.

Picking up the axe, he pounded the can until it split. Raging against this wasteland that had trapped him, and the fate that had stripped him of his wings, he furiously shovelled the cold mess into his mouth and choked it down.

Konala sat watching him intently. When he had finished she rose to her feet, pointed northward and asked, "*Peehuktuk?* We walk?"

Lavery's resentment exploded. Thrusting his arms through the straps of the packsack, he heaved it and the sleeping bag into position then picked up the rifle and pointed with it to the southwest.

"You're goddamn right!" he shouted. "Me—*owunga peehuktuk* that way! *Eeetpeet*—you bloody well stay here!"

Without waiting to see if she had understood, he began to climb the slope of a sandy esker that rose to the south of the pond. Near the crest he paused and looked back. Konala was squatting by the tiny fire seemingly unaware that he was deserting her. He felt a momentary twinge of guilt, but shrugged it off . . . no way she could make it with him to Baker, and she had her deerskins to keep her warm. As for food, well, Huskies could eat anything . . . she'd make out. He turned and his long, ungainly figure passed over the skyline.

With a chill of dismay he looked out across the tundra rolling to a measureless horizon ahead of him —a curving emptiness more intimidating than any-

138

thing he had seen in the high skies. The tongue of fear began to flicker again but he resolutely shut his mind to it and stumbled forward into that sweep of space, his heavy flight boots slipping on rocks and sucking in the muskeg, the straps of the packsack already cutting into his shoulders through the thin cotton jacket.

There is no way of knowing what Konala was thinking as she saw him go. She might have believed he was going hunting, since that would have been the natural thing for a man to do under the circumstances. But in all likelihood she guessed what he intended—otherwise, how to explain the fact that ten days later and nearly sixty miles to the south of the downed plane, the sick woman trudged wearily across a waste of sodden muskeg to climb a gravel ridge and halt beside the unconscious body of Charlie Lavery?

Squatting beside him she used her curved knife to cut away the useless remnants of his leather boots, then wrapped his torn and bloody feet in compresses of wet sphagnum moss. Slipping off her parka, she spread it over his tattered jacket to protect him from the flies. Her fingers on his emaciated and insect-bitten flesh were tender and sure. Later she built a fire, and when Lavery opened his eyes it was to find himself under a rude skin shelter with a can of fish broth being pressed lightly against his lips.

There was a hiatus in his mind. Anxiously he raised himself to see if the aircraft was still on the pond, but there was no pond and no old Anson . . . only that same stunning expanse of empty plains. With a sickening lurch, memory began to function. The seemingly endless days of his journey flooded back upon him: filled with roaring clouds of mosquitoes and flies; with a mounting, driving hunger; the agony of lacerated feet and the misery of rain-swept hours lying shelterless in a frigid void. He remembered his matches getting soaked when he tried to ford the first of a succession of rivers that forever deflected his course toward the west. He remembered losing the .22 cartridges when the box turned to mush after a rain. Above all, he remembered the unbearable sense of loneliness that grew until he began to panic, throwing away first the useless gun, then the sodden sleeping bag, the axe . . . and finally sent him, in a heart-bursting spasm of desperation, toward a stony ridge that seemed to undulate serpent-like on the otherwise shapeless face of a world that had lost all form and substance.

Konala's face came into focus as she nudged the tin against his lips. She was smiling and Lavery found himself smiling weakly back at this woman who not so long before had roused his contempt and anger.

They camped on the nameless ridge for a week while Lavery recovered some of his strength. At first he could hardly bear to leave the shelter because of the pain in his feet. But Konala seemed always on the move: gathering willow twigs for fires, collecting and cooking food, cutting and sewing a new pair of boots for Lavery from the hides she had brought with her. She appeared tireless, but that was an illusion. Her body was driven to its many tasks only at great cost.

Time had telescoped itself so that Lavery would wake from sleep with shaking hands, hearing the engines of the Anson fail. It would seem to him that the plane had crashed only a few minutes earlier. It would seem that the terrible ordeal of his march south was about to begin again and he would feel a sick return of panic. When this happened, he would desperately fix his thoughts on Konala for she was the one comforting reality in all this alien world.

He thought about her a great deal, but she was an enigma to him. Sick as she was, how had she managed to follow him across those sodden plains and broken rock ridges . . . how had she managed to keep alive in such a country?

After Konala gave him the completed skin boots carefully lined with cotton grass, he began to find answers to some of these questions. He was able to hobble far enough from camp to watch her set sinew snares for gaudy ground squirrels she called *hikik*, scoop suckers from a nearby stream with her bare hands, outrun snow geese that were still flightless after the late-summer moult, and dig succulent lemmings from their peat bog burrows. Watching her, Lavery slowly came to understand that what had seemed to him a lifeless desert was in fact a land generous in its support of those who knew its nature.

Still, the most puzzling question remained unanswered. Why had Konala not stayed in the relative safety of the aircraft or else travelled north to seek her own people? What had impelled her to follow him . . . to rescue a man of another race who had abandoned her?

Toward the end of their stay on the ridge, the sun was beginning to dip well below the horizon at night—a warning that summer was coming to an end. One day Konala again pointed north and, with a grin, she waddled duck-like a few paces in that direction. The joke at the expense of Lavery's splayed and painful feet did not annoy him. He laughed and limped after her to show his willingness to follow wherever she might lead.

When they broke camp, Konala insisted on carrying what was left of Lavery's gear along with her own pouch and the roll of caribou hides which was both shelter and bedding for them. As they trekked

141

northward she broke into song—a high and plaintive chant without much melody which seemed as much part of the land as the fluting of curlews. When Lavery tried to find out what the song was all about, she seemed oddly reticent and all he could gather was that she was expressing kinship for someone or for some thing beyond his ken. He did not understand that she was joining her voice to the voice of the land and to the spirits of the land.

Retracing their path under Konala's tutelage became a journey of discovery. Lavery was forever being surprised at how different the tundra had now become from the dreadful void he had trudged across not long since.

He discovered it was full of birds ranging from tiny longspurs whose muted colouring made them almost invisible, to great saffron-breasted hawks circling high above the bogs and lakes. Konala also drew his attention to the endless diversity of tundra plants, from livid orange lichens to azure flowers whose blooms were so tiny he had to kneel to see them clearly.

Once Konala motioned him to crawl beside her to the crest of an esker. In the valley beyond, a family of white wolves was lazily hunting lemmings in a patch of sedge a hundred feet away. The nearness of the big beasts made Lavery uneasy until Konala boldly stood up and called to the wolves in their own language. They drew together then, facing her in a half circle, and answered with a long, lilting chorus before trotting away in single file.

Late one afternoon they at last caught sight of a splash of brilliant colour in the distance. Lavery's heartbeat quickened and he pushed forward without regard for his injured feet. The yellow-painted Anson *might* have been spotted by a search plane during their absence . . . rescue by his own kind might still be possible. But when the man and woman descended the esker to the shore of the pond, they found the Anson exactly as they had left it. There had been no human visitors.

Bitterly disappointed, Lavery climbed into the cockpit, seated himself behind the controls and slumped into black depression. Konala's intention of travelling northward to rejoin her own people on the coast now loomed as an ordeal whose outcome would probably be death during the first winter storm . . . if they could last that long. Their worn clothing and almost hairless robes were already barely adequate to keep the cold at bay. Food was getting harder to find as the birds left, the small animals began to dig in and the fish ran back to the sea. And what about fuel when the weather really began to turn against them?

Lavery was sullen and silent that evening as they ate their boiled fish, but Konala remained cheerful. She kept repeating the word *tuktu*—caribou—as she vainly tried to make him understand that soon they would have the wherewithal to continue the journey north.

As the night wind began to rise he ignored the skin shelter which Konala had erected and, taking one of the robes, climbed back into the plane and rolled himself up on the icy metal floor. During the next few days he spent most of his time in the Anson, sometimes fiddling with the knobs of the useless radio, but for the most part morosely staring through the Plexiglass windscreen at a landscape which seemed to grow increasingly bleak as the first frosts greyed the tundra flowers and browned the windswept sedges.

Early one morning an unfamiliar sound brought him out of a chilled, nightmarish sleep. It was a muffled, subdued noise as of waves rolling in on a distant shore. For one heart-stopping instant he thought it was the beat of an aircraft engine, then he heard Konala's exultant cry.

"*Tuktoraikayai*—the deer have come!"

From the window of the dead machine Lavery looked out upon a miracle of life. An undulating mass of antlered animals was pouring out of the north. It rolled steadily toward the pond, split, and began enveloping it. The rumble resolved itself into a rattling cadence of hooves on rock and gravel. As the animals swept past, the stench of barnyard grew strong even inside the plane. Although in the days when he had flown high above them Lavery had often seen skeins of migrating caribou laced across the arctic plains like a pattern of beaded threads, he could hardly credit what he now beheld . . . the land inundated under a veritable flood of life. His depression began to dissipate as he felt himself being drawn into and becoming almost a part of that living river.

While he stared, awe-struck and incredulous, Konala went to work. Some days earlier she had armed herself with a spear, its shaft made from a paddle she had found in the Anson and its double-edged blade filed out of a piece of steel broken from the tip of the plane's anchor. With this in hand she was now scurrying about on the edge of the herd. The press was so great that individual deer could not avoid her. A snorting buck leapt high as the spear drove into him just behind the ribs. His dying leap carried him onto the backs of some of his neighbours, and as he slid off and disappeared into the ruck, Konala's blade thrust into another victim. She chose the fattest beasts and those with the best hides.

When the tide of caribou finally thinned, there was much work for Konala's knife. She skinned, scraped and staked out several prime hides destined for the making of clothes and sleeping robes, then turned her attention to a small mountain of meat and began slicing it into paper-thin sheets which she draped over dwarf willow bushes. When dry this would make light, imperishable food fit to sustain a man and woman—one injured and the other sick—who must undertake a long, demanding journey.

Revitalized by the living ambience of the great herd, Lavery came to help her. She glanced up at him and her face was radiant. She cut off a piece of brisket and held it out to him, grinning delightedly when he took it and tore off a piece with his teeth. It was his idea to make a stove out of two empty oil cans upon which the fat which Konala had gathered could be rendered into white cakes that would provide food *and* fuel in the times ahead.

Several days of brisk, clear weather followed. While the meat dried on the bushes, Konala laboured on, cutting and stitching clothing for them both. She worked herself so hard that her cheeks again showed the flame of fever and her rasping cough grew worse. When Lavery tried to make her take things a little easier she became impatient with him. Konala knew what she knew.

Finally on a day in mid-September she decided they were ready. With Lavery limping at her side, she turned her back on the white men's fine machine and set out to find her people.

The skies darkened and cold gales began sweeping gusts of snow across the bogs whose surfaces were already crusting with ice crystals. One day a sleet storm forced them into early camp. Konala had left the little travel tent to gather willows for the fire and Lavery was dozing when he heard her cry of warning through the shrilling of the wind.

There was no mistaking the urgency in her voice.

Snatching up the spear he limped from the tent to see Konala running across a narrow valley. Behind her, looming immense and forbidding in the leaden light, was one of the great brown bears of the barrenlands.

Seeing Lavery poised on the slope above her, Konala swerved away, even though this brought her closer to the bear. It took a moment for Lavery to realize that she was attempting to distract the beast, then he raised the spear and flung himself down the slope, shouting and cursing at the top of his lungs.

The bear's interest in the woman shifted to the surprising spectacle Lavery presented. It sat up on its massive haunches and peered doubtfully at him through the veil of sleet.

When he was a scant few yards from the bear, Lavery tripped and fell, rolling helplessly among the rocks to fetch up on his back staring upward into that huge, square face. The bear looked back impassively then snorted, dropped on all fours and shambled off.

The meeting with the bear crystallized the changes which had been taking place in Lavery. Clad in caribou-skin clothing, a dark beard ringing his cheeks, and his hair hanging free to his shoulders, he had acquired a look of litheness and vigour—and of watchfulness. No longer was he an alien in an inimical land. He was a man now in his own right, able to make his way in an elder world.

In Konala's company he knew a unity that he had previously felt only with members of his bombing crew. The weeks they had spent together had eroded the barrier of language and he was beginning to understand much about her that had earlier baffled him. Yet the core of the enigma remained for he had not found the answer to the question that had haunted him since she brought life back to his body on that distant southern ridge.

For some time they had been descending an already frozen and snow-covered river which Konala had given him to understand would lead them to the coast. But with each passing day, Konala had been growing weaker even as Lavery regained his strength. At night, when she supposed him to be asleep, she sometimes moaned softly, and during the day she could walk only for short distances between paroxysms of coughing that left blood stains in the new snow at her feet.

When the first real blizzard struck them, it was Lavery who set up the travel tent and lit the fire of lichens and caribou fat upon which to simmer some dried deer meat. Konala lay under their sleeping robes while he prepared the meal, and when he turned to her he saw how the lines of pain around her mouth had deepened into crevices. He came close and held a tin of warm soup to her dry lips. She drank a mouthful then lay back, her dark eyes glittering too brightly in the meagre firelight. He looked deep into them and read the confirmation of his fear.

Keeping her eyes on his, she took a new pair of skin boots from under the robes and slowly stroked them, feeling the infinitely fine stitching which would keep them waterproof. After a time she reached out and placed them in his lap. Then she spoke, slowly and carefully so he would be sure to understand.

"They are not very good boots but they might carry you to the camps of my people. They might help you return to your own land. . . . Walk well in them . . . my brother."

Later that night the gale rose to a crescendo. The cold drove into the tent and, ignoring the faint flicker of the fire, pierced through the thick caribou robes wrapped about Konala and entered into her.

When the storm had blown itself out, Lavery buried her under a cairn of rocks on the high banks of the nameless river. As he made his way northward in the days that followed, his feet finding their own sure way, he no longer pondered the question which had lain in his mind through so many weeks . . . for he could still hear the answer she had made and would forever hear it: Walk well . . . my brother. . . .

The White Canoe

Desolation enveloped the tundra. The treeless plains stretching to an illimitable horizon all around me seemed neither land nor water but a nebulous blend of both. No birds flew in the overcast skies and no beasts moved on the dun-coloured waste of bog. A grey cloud scud driving low over gravel ridges bore the chill of snow. All visible life seemed to have fled, as I too was fleeing, before the thrust of approaching winter.

I had already been travelling for three weeks down the River and had seen no sign of any other human beings. Fear that I might never escape from this uninhabited wilderness grew as my battered canoe leapt and writhed in the torrent as if afflicted with its own panic. The River was one long sequence of roaring white water that had early taken toll. My rifle, pack and winter clothing together with most of my grub had been lost in the first furious rapids four hundred miles to the westward.

Half starved, with no more than a few handfuls of wet flour remaining for my body's sustenance, and soaked by spume and spray, I was sinking into apathy from which, on some wild rapid still to come, I might not be able to rouse myself in time.

The River whipped me around one of its angled bends to face a mighty ridge rising powerfully out of the sodden tundra like an island in a frozen sea. It should have been visible from many miles upstream yet I had seen nothing of it until the current flung me up against its flank. I had an overwhelming desire to feel its solid stone beneath my feet. Thrusting my paddle against the oily muscles of the current, I came panting to the shore.

When I reached the top of that great mound, I halted abruptly. Before me lay an immense white canoe upended on a bed of frost-shattered granite and shining like a monument of quartz. It had been so placed to leave a narrow opening between the gunwale and the bed rock. Kneeling, I peered into the gloom and could just make out the outlines of many shapes and bundles. Joyfully I thought, and perhaps spoke aloud, "It's got to be a cache!" My strength was just sufficient to lift the gunwale a few more inches and wedge it up with a fragment of rock so I could reach one arm underneath.

The first thing I touched and drew toward me was a .50 Sharps rifle swathed in rotted deerskins and so well coated in hardened tallow that there was not a speck of rust on it. Further scrabbling produced two boxes of shells, their brass cases green with verdigris, but their powder dry; a gill net complete with floats and sinkers; and a bleached wooden box holding several pounds of tea and half a dozen plugs of tobacco.

There were also fish spears, steel traps, snowknives, cooking pots and other implements of an Eskimo household, together with a number of nameless packages which seemed to have succumbed to mildew and decay and which I assumed held bedding and clothing of caribou and muskox fur.

I had no hesitation in taking the things I needed. It seemed clear enough that the Eskimo who had made this cache had done so long ago and had never returned to it nor ever would.

The gifts of the white canoe included the knowledge that my escape from the void of the barrenland plains was now reasonably certain. Where this great craft, coming inland from the coast, had been able to ascend against the River, there my canoe could surely descend. The sea—deliverance—*must* be close. Yet when I walked to the eastern end of the ridge and looked eagerly beyond it, I could see nothing except the cold undulations of that same sodden plain in which I had been imprisoned for so long. Escape still lay somewhere beyond a grey horizon blurring into darkness under an onslaught of driven rain.

I carted my loot back to the river edge, set the net in a backwater and returned to shore to make a little fire of willow twigs on which to brew up a huge pail of tea. As I sat by the minute flames, I mused upon the presence of the white canoe, invisible now in the darkness looming over me.

That it had lain on the ridge for decades past I could not doubt. The decay beneath it, and the way the meagre lichens had grown around it, proved this must be so. Yet the canoe itself seemed to have denied the years. Its flanks were smooth, unmarred by summer rains or winter gales. Its wood was sound and as dry and hard as iron. It was of a sea-going type built especially for the Hudson's Bay Company trade and much favoured by Eskimos along the arctic coasts. But what was it doing here?

Rain hissed over the roiling waters and winked out my fire. I crawled into my robes, pulled a canvas tarp over me and went to sleep.

In the icy dawn I lifted the net and found it heavy with trout and grayling. After cooking my first real meal in many days, I committed myself to the River again.

For five more days I travelled down that watery slope, portaging or running rapids, always straining toward the sea. On the first day I saw a lone caribou on the bank, a straggler left behind by the south-bound migrating herds. The old Sharps roared like the voice of doom, nearly knocking me out of the canoe; and that night I gorged on fresh and bloody meat.

On the evening of the fifth day, the River slowed and widened into a long lake. There was a low, rocky island in its centre, upon whose shores two deerskin tents squatted like miniature volcanic cones upon a long-dead lava bed.

I made toward them and a mob of dogs broke into a furious uproar, bringing a handful of people tumbling out of the tents. The men waded into the icy shallows to the top of their waterproof skin boots and drew my canoe to shore. We were all overcome with a childlike shyness.

Although I had lived with Eskimos in the past, it had been weeks since I had spoken to any other human being; and coming as I did from the uninhabited plains to the west, my appearance must have seemed as inexplicable to these people as any shooting star across the midnight sky.

They were six in number. There was an old man,

Katalak, whose face had been corroded by the long years into a gargoyle mask; and his wife, Salak, also withered with age but still sharp-eyed and alert. There was their stolid middle-aged son, Haluk; his plump wife, Petuk, and their two children, Okak and Akoomik.

They escorted me into Katalak's tent and, while the women lit a willow fire outside and brought a pot of deer tongues to the boil, we three men sat on a pile of skins and smoked. They asked no questions although their curiosity about me must have been intense.

After we had fed and drunk a gallon or so of tea, I explained that I had come down the River from its source, which I had reached after a twenty-day journey north from timberline. They told me that none of their people had ever lived or travelled that far to the west except for one who had gone that way a long, long time ago and never returned.

"Perhaps I know something of him," I said, and I told of finding the cache under the white canoe and how the things I had taken from it had probably saved my life.

A silence followed, during which Katalak carefully filled the soapstone bowl of his pipe, lit it, puffed once then passed it to his wife. Eventually he spoke.

"The white canoe is no man's cache. It is the spirit home of Kakut, who was my father and who is the father of us all."

I was appalled by my own stupidity, for I had known that, in death, pagan Eskimos take with them the things they have found necessary during their earthly lives. I knew now that instead of borrowing from a cache, I had robbed a grave.

Katalak sensed my distress. He stretched out his

hand and laid it lightly on my shoulder. The expression on his seamed and desiccated face was reassuring.

"You did no wrong," he said gently. "Had Kakut wished otherwise, you would have travelled past the hill called Kinetua and seen nothing. You took from his grave only what he was glad to give."

He reloaded the pipe and when it was lit he passed it to me. Darkness had fallen and Salak brought a small tin can filled with caribou fat into which a wick of wild cotton had been inserted. This lamp produced a meagre, reddish flame that wavered beneath a pennant of black smoke. In that flickering and faint illumination I could just see the old man's face, shadowed but intent. He looked slowly at each in turn, until his gaze rested on me.

"You are *Kablunait*, a white man. We are *Innuit*, the People. But tonight we are as one. None of us would be here if Kakut had not wished it so. We live, all of us, because of gifts made by dead hands. There is a story to tell about that."

In the time long ago, I lived by the River, and my father was Kakut, and his name was known along the sea coast and up all the rivers far into the plains that belonged to the deer, the muskox, and the great brown bear. Many mysteries were known to Kakut—mysteries that belonged to the Woman in the days when she made Men. Kakut spoke with the spirits. His hunting fed entire camps during bad times, and hunger never came into the tents and snowhouses where he lived. *Ai-ee!* He was a man who knew how to give the spirits their due.

He was such a powerful man that I lived under his shadow, and because of that I was not content. In my sixteenth summer I accompanied my family to the coast for the yearly trading, but when they went back up the River I did not go with them for I had begun to listen to other voices. There were new Gods in the land who spoke through the black-bearded white men you call priests. One of these had built an igloo of wood near the trader and, during our visit, he spoke often to me and told me many strange things. He also talked to the trader, asking him to give me work for the winter so I could stay in that place and learn the ways and the thoughts of the white men.

The trader was uneasy about that because he knew the power of Kakut and had no wish to anger him. So I went to my father and told him what I desired. He did not stand in my way. "The young wolf runs where he runs," was all he said.

I stayed for two years with the white men and learned to speak a new language. But my blood still remembered the old tongues, and when Salak came down to the coast during my eighteenth summer, the old tongues outshouted the new. I wished her to become my woman and stay with me and learn white men's ways. We would possess ourselves, I told her, of the many good things the white men have, and live in a wooden igloo and be always warm and well fed. Salak agreed to become my woman and she came to live with me but she would not agree to stay at the coast. In the autumn she moved into the tent of my father and his family and prepared to return up the River with them. She said that our child-to-be was of the Innuit, not of the Kablunait, and he must be born in his own land among his own people. I was angry with her but, also, I loved her very much and so, against my desires, I gave up the life at the coast and went with my family and my wife.

That winter I thought my own thoughts but did not speak them aloud. It was not until the dark days of mid-winter, when my mother died and they made ready to place her under the rocks with the tools, clothing and ornaments which were hers, that I could no longer be quiet.

Then I spoke out against the foolishness of burying all those good things with the dead. I told those who sat about in my father's snowhouse it was evil to take the wealth that comes so hard to our people and place it on the windswept rocks to bleach and blow into decay. The women moaned and bent their bodies, and the men turned from me and would not look in my direction. All save Kakut.

His face alone did not change when I spoke against the ways of my people; and he replied in a voice that was as soft as the whisper of the white owl's wings.

"*Eeee* . . . those are words you have said. Perhaps they are the words of one who has darkness in front of his eyes. Men become blind when they travel over new snow on a day when there is a haze over the sun, and that happens because they deny the powers that lie in the wind and the snow and the sky and the sun. That is one kind of darkness. There is another. It comes when men deny or forget what their fathers' fathers knew. We must pity you, Katalak, for you are blind."

After that, I found I could no longer remain in the camps of my people. One day I harnessed my dogs and I took Salak and forced her onto my sled and drove my sled east to the coast and back to the place where the white men lived. Salak made no complaint but did her woman's work while I worked for the trader and became almost his right hand. In the spring, when the snow geese returned to the ponds by the coast, she gave birth.

So did we live until three years after my Haluk was born. That summer, when the families who made up the camp of my father arrived as usual at the coast, I saw that one canoe was missing. It was the great white canoe that belonged to my father.

I went to the camp of the newcomers, and I knew all of the people. They gave me greetings and I waited, as is the custom, for them to tell what was new. They were slow to speak and I grew impatient and asked a straight question, which was a rude thing to do. Someone answered, "It is true. Kakut is dead."

Then I spoke words whose memory will shame me forever.

"Well, then . . . if my father is dead, where is his canoe? Where are his rifles and the many fine things which were his? I am Katalak, his son, and it is just that the son should have those things, for the son is alive and has mouths to feed."

Those people gave me no answer. They spoke of the hard winter, of the shortage of white foxes, of many things which did not concern me, but of my father's possessions they would not speak.

That night I talked to Salak. I told her we would borrow the trader's canoe and engine—he had the first engine ever seen in the country—and we would go back up the River and find the grave of my father. Then I would have those things which the priest and the trader said were rightfully mine, and I would use them and not leave them to rot over the bones of a man who no longer could have any needs.

Salak replied that I would do what I would do but, as for her, she wanted for nothing nor did she think she and I and Haluk, and the child who was soon to be born, wanted for anything. She was content, she said, and it would be well if we were all

157

content. But I would not listen to the words of a woman for to have done so would have shamed me in the eyes of the white men.

We began our journey next day. The River was deserted in that season because the people had all come down to the coast to trade, to escape the flies and to fish. We had a good eighteen-foot canoe and the little engine, and for awhile all went well. We climbed slowly westward up the white waters. Then the engine broke down and I did not know how to fix it. The flies became a black plague such as I had never known before. The deer, which should have been travelling with their fawns in small companies all over the tundra, seemed to have vanished, and we ran out of food. We had to track the canoe up the rapids for Haluk was too young to help and Salak too pregnant and I could not portage it alone.

But I would not give up. And so we came at last to the camp where I had been born and found no sign of the grave of Kakut. I left Haluk and Salak there, scraping moss off the rocks in order to eat, and went westward on foot. I walked for three days by the banks of the River and found nothing.

When I got back to the camp Salak was sick. We turned back toward the sea, but before we came to the coast Salak gave birth to a dead child—a son it was—and she buried the body in the old way, under some rocks by the shore. I said nothing when she took tea and tobacco and wrapped these things in her own parka and placed them on top of the grave.

That journey should have ended the matter and perhaps it would have done so, but during the following winter a stranger came to the trading post. He was of the *Padliermiut* who dwell far to the northwest and seldom come out to the coast. This man had made the long journey to try and buy ammunition, for his people were out of powder and lead and were starving. His had been a very hard journey and he had been forced to kill most of his dogs. Finally he became lost in strange country and was so weak from hunger he could not go on.

Then, so he told us, he saw a mountain appear high and black on the bleak plains where, before, he had seen nothing. On its crest he saw something white. Although he was afraid, for he was sure this was a vision of the kind men see when death is upon them, he approached and saw a big white canoe. When he went near it, he found the fat carcass of an autumn-killed deer lying on the windswept ridge, its body untouched by foxes or wolves. He took that meat and fed himself and his two remaining dogs, and then followed the frozen path of the River east to the coast.

When he told his story some people talked of the helping spirits. I paid them no heed, but when the stranger spoke of the great white canoe I listened. He described where it lay and where the mountain was. Then I thought he was lying, for in my search I had walked far up the River and had seen no mountain. Even so, I was sure he had found the grave of my father and would return to it on his way back to his own people and take from it the goods which were mine.

That evening I hitched up the post dogs and set off on the stranger's back trail. There was need for haste because the first gale would cover his tracks, so I drove the dogs and myself without mercy. Strangely, the weather stayed calm for a week and the tracks left by the sled of the stranger remained as clear as when he made them.

It was after dark when I came to the place where he said he had seen the great ridge. I waited for dawn, but before it could come a blizzard began to blow out of the north. It blew for five days, keeping me trapped in a hole I had dug in the drift, with no heat and no light and my food almost gone.

On the fifth day the wind changed and blew hard enough from the west to cover the land with ground drift so that nothing could be seen. I was driven east out of the plains as a puff of water is driven out of a whale's head when he spouts.

When I got back to the settlement, the trader was angry because I had gone away without his permission and because the post dogs were starved and their feet cut to pieces. He called me a fool. He said the rich grave of my father did not really exist—that it was no more than a story invented to hide from me the fact that the rifles and traps, the nets and the tools of Kakut, had been stolen as soon as he died. The priest said the same thing, adding these words, "Your people are liars and thieves. They are pagans, and cannot be believed. Only when God has come into their hearts will you get back what is rightfully yours."

I believed what the white men said and for years my heart was bitter against my own people. Whenever they came to the post I would make an opportunity to examine their gear. Although I never recognized anything which had belonged to my father, this meant to me only that the people feared discovery and had left the stolen things cached in the country when they came to the coast.

For ten more years I lived with the white men, doing their work and trying to be like them. I tried hard to forget the ways of my people. I thought each new year would be the one when I would cease to be of the Innuit and become truly one of the Kablunait— for this was what they had promised would come to pass if I remained with them and did as they wished.

But the years drew on, and Haluk was growing toward manhood, and Salak bore no more children and there was no change in my life. The people who came to trade at the post treated me distantly, as if I was one of the white men; but the white men did not treat me as one of themselves. Sometimes it seemed that Salak and Haluk and I were alone in the world, and I began to have very bad dreams. I dreamt I was alone in a deserted place where no birds sang, no wolves howled, nothing moved except me, and the sky was growing darker and darker, and I knew that when the night came it would never be followed by another dawn.

I began to grow silent and I did not laugh, and my wife was afraid for me. One day she took courage and spoke.

"My husband, let us go away from this place and return to the River and to the people. For laughter is there, and the deer walk the land, and fish swim in the waters."

Her words were very painful to me so I took my dog whip and struck her across the face with the butt of it, and she was silent.

The months passed and my heart was rotting within me, but I would not turn my face to the River for I could not go back to the people who had stolen what was mine. Yet sometimes, after I dreamt the terrible dreams, I saw their faces in the darkness and they were smiling and their lips shaped words of welcome that I could not hear.

One day the priest came to the wooden shanty in which we lived.

"Katalak," he said, "you have long wished to be one of us—of the Kablunait—now the time is coming. When the trading ship arrives in the summer it will take your son, Haluk, away in it and he will go to

161

the world where all men are white men. He will stay there many years and will learn many things, and when he returns to this land he will be a God-man and like a Kablunait, and so, through him, you will become one of us too."

So he spoke, but instead of bringing me peace his words filled me with despair. Something swelled in my chest and almost throttled me. A shrieking voice swept through my mind. I picked up my snow-knife, swung it high over my head and ran at him, shouting: "This you shall not do! You have had *my* life! It is enough! You will not have Haluk's too!"

The priest fled, but in a little while he came back accompanied by the trader. Both carried rifles, and the trader pointed his rifle at my belly and told me he was going to lock me in the dark cellar where we kept the walrus meat for the dogs. He called me a mur-derer and told me the police would come in the sum-mer and I would be punished for a long time. He was so angry, spit fell from his mouth. But I was even an-grier. I reached again for the snowknife, and then he fired and the bullet went into me just under my ribs.

After that there is a space of many days I do not remember. When I came to myself I was in my cousin Powaktuk's canoe. With me was my son and my wife and Powaktuk's family. I was lying on some deerskin robes. I could only raise my head a little but I could see over the gunwales and I knew where we were. We were going up the River. I was being carried back to the place of my people.

When they saw I was awake they smiled at me and nodded their heads, and my cousin said, "It comes to pass. On the day Kakut died he spoke, say-ing that after his eyes became blind forever the eyes of his son would see again."

It had taken a long time for my father's words to begin to come true.

As we continued up the River we stopped at many camps and everywhere I was welcomed back to the land. At each camp people gave me things. Some gave me dogs, some gave me traps, one gave me a good rifle. Another gave me a sled, another a set of harness, and yet another gave Salak a fine meat tray. So it went until by the time we reached this island and prepared to make our own camp, Salak and Haluk and I wanted for nothing with which to begin the old life again.

My cousin and his family camped with us and everyone took such good care of me that I was able to walk before the first snows came. The deer arrived in greater numbers than anyone could remember and we cached enough meat and fat to keep us and the dogs well fed until spring. We set our traps and there were many foxes, and life was good in this place.

One night when the blizzard thundered, I sat in my cousin's snowhouse and spoke to him of certain things which had lain within me for a long time.

"I am a man whose liver is eaten by shame," I told him. "Through all the years since Kakut died I believed the people had taken for themselves the things which were my father's. Now I know they only kept those things against the day of my return. Shame has eaten my liver, yet there is one thing I would like to know. Where is Kakut's great canoe? When the ice goes from the River I will have need of a canoe of my own."

My cousin looked at me strangely.

"Eeee, Katalak, the blindness has not yet left your inner eye; otherwise you would have seen that of all the things that you have in your snowhouse, none is familiar from your father's time. You have forgotten, perhaps, that what one of us has belongs to all of us in time of need. These things are true gifts made to you in your time of need. As for the white canoe, it lies where it has lain since Kakut's death— over his bones and over all the things he had in life and which he may have need of in the place beyond.'"

When I heard this I was more ashamed than ever, yet I felt better inside myself too, for now there was no one else to blame for the mistake I had made when I abandoned my people. There was only myself left to be angry with. And why should a man be angry with himself?

Throughout that winter I slowly learned to live without anger, and it was the best winter of my life. All the people in that camp were as one, and I was again part of that one. Sometimes people from other camps came to visit with us, and sometimes we drove down the River to visit them. There were song-feasts and there was story telling and much eating of good meat. Then in the middle of the winter Salak began to grow big with child. It seemed to me that at last I had everything a man could want, and the memory of the years when I had wished to be one of the Kablunait began to grow dim, like the spirit lights in the northern sky fading into the brightness as the spring returns to the land.

When the sun began to climb high over the horizon and the snows started to soften, we finished with our trapping and made ready to receive the returning deer herds.

This island where we sit is a fine place for deer hunting because it is like a stepping stone in the middle of the long lake. In the autumn the deer herds heading south swim to it and rest before continuing on their way. Heading north in the spring, they cross

164

over to it on the ice, for they remember it and take the same path they used in the autumn. Also the island has stands of willows to provide us with fuel, so it is a good place to camp. But in the spring when the ice grows black and rotten and the River begins to break up, we must leave it for then sometimes the island is flooded. It is our custom to camp on the mainland shore at that time of the year until we can begin our voyage down to the coast by canoe.

In the spring that I speak of, the winter snows lay very thick on the land; and when the thaws started, the water flowed everywhere across the rocks and swamps as if the land itself was melting. My cousin and I saw it would be a year of big floods so one day we sledded his canoe over to the mainland shore and cached it at a safe height above the still-frozen surface of the river. Then we returned to the island intending to take all the people and goods ashore on the sleds the following day.

That was our plan, but during the night the spirits sent us such a storm as I do not ever remember seeing. It began with a fall of wet snow, then the wind rose and the snow turned to rain that poured out of the night as if Sredna, Mistress of the Waters, had turned her world upside down. Our snowhouse crumbled and when I tried to stretch caribou hides over the holes the wind was so strong it brought me to my knees. Then the howl of the wind was lost in a shuddering thunder that shook the roots of the island. We knew what it was. Swollen with the flood from the land, the River had risen and burst free of the ice. Swirling floes, thicker than the height of a man, were being flung out over the rotten surface ice of the lake, crushing our road to the shore.

I shouted for my cousin but my voice was snatched away by the wind and lost in the roaring as

165

the islands of ice beat each other to pieces. Salak and Haluk and I fought our way toward a high drift in whose lee my cousin's snowhouse had stood. We met him and his family crawling toward us. His house had collapsed. We all managed to burrow into the back of the soaking-wet drift, and there we stayed until dawn.

It came grey and ugly, whipped by a rain that seemed to grow steadily worse. We knew the rain on the half-melted snows would make the River swell ever faster. Yet with the return of the daylight, our courage came back. We gathered most of our things on the highest part of the island and set up a tent. We had plenty of food, and we believed the lake could hardly rise high enough to submerge the whole island. We believed we had only to wait four or five days for the flooding to end, then we would find some way to escape.

All day we sat in the low tent around a small, smoky fire of wet willow and caribou fat, and we were not frightened. It is not the way of the people to worry when trouble comes. We laughed at our plight, and told stories. Haluk was wild with excitement for he was hardly more than a boy and this was an adventure he would remember through the long years ahead.

It was Haluk who brought the bad news. During a lull in the rain he had gone to the head of the island to watch the floes spinning past. In a little while he was back, running as hard as he could and shouting, "Come quick! Come quick! The island is sinking!"

When we hurried down to the shore we found the lake waters rising so fast they had already covered the slope where the dogs were tethered, and the beasts were up to their bellies, frantically pulling against their leads. We waded in and freed them, but the water continued to rise so swiftly that we were bewildered, not understanding why the water was rising so fast. It was my cousin who guessed the answer.

"It must be the rapids at the foot of the lake," he said. "They have held the pack ice. The gorge must be plugged and now the River has nowhere to go!"

Then we knew we had little time. If the gorge stayed blocked the lake would rise until the island vanished beneath those cold waters.

The women made haste to pack all our important possessions into small bundles after which they placed the heavy things, traps, cooking pots and such, in a hole over which they rolled big rocks. As for my cousin and me, our thoughts were racing, but we could think of no way to flee from the island. Our people do not swim, and in any case no swimmer could have escaped being crushed by the pounding fragments of ice. Nor could we ride the ice pans as one would a raft, for the turmoil was so great and the wind so strong that not even the largest floes were safe from upsetting or being overswept by other floes. I wondered if we might build an *umiak*, a woman's boat of the kind sometimes used by the coastal people, out of willow branches and caribou skins, but I knew there was no time for that.

It seemed we could do nothing but hope that the dam in the gorge would soon burst. I stood on the highest place and saw that the waters had already swallowed more than half the island.

Then it was as if I became two persons. I was a man of my people, but standing beside me was another self. It was a very strange thing that happened. One of my beings was calm, feeling no fear, and this was one who had come back to his own place. The other was panic-stricken, mouthing the prayers he had been taught by the priest.

I was two beings who struggled against each

other; and it was the man of the people who won. He felt such a contempt for that other that he flung him away, and he vanished into the cold ice-mist that swirled over the lake. Then I was alone and I looked about me at the world that had harboured my people since time before memory, and I was content to be there even though I believed the waters must soon make an end of us all. I thought of Kakut, and inside myself I asked him to take me back.

These are true things I am speaking; and it is a true thing that when I lifted my eyes to look westward toward the place where my father lay, I saw his canoe.

I saw that great canoe, whiter than the ice around it, breasting the heaving waters and driving down upon the island's head.

I was still watching as if it was something seen in a dream when Haluk ran up the slope and seized my arm. His young voice was shrill and it pierced into the quiet places in my mind. He yelled at me and pulled hard on my arm, and my vision cleared and I went with him.

My cousin and the rest of the people were also running toward the head of the island, everyone burdened with bundles and surrounded by the half-crazy dogs. We were ready when the great canoe grounded. Everything was swiftly loaded. Everyone climbed aboard and there was still room to spare, for Kakut's canoe was a mighty one.

The crossing to the mainland was not easily made and there were times when it seemed certain the canoe would be crushed and all of us drowned. But it was not crushed, and we escaped from the island.

The old man ceased telling his story. Haluk's wife, Petuk, went outside, blew up the embers of the fire, and began to boil another pail of tea. After awhile I went down to where my canoe lay. I took from it the rifle, the remaining shells, the net and the tea and tobacco and brought them back to the tent. Katalak looked up as I lifted the flap . . . he looked up and after a moment he smiled so broadly it seemed all the years had lifted from his face. Then they were all laughing. Katalak reached over and poked me in the ribs.

"One time I saw a wolf that looked as hungry as you, all bones and a bit of dry skin. He lost his teeth somehow. *Eh!* I think you lost your teeth on the River. Well, Kakut gave them back and you had better keep them until you get to the coast. Leave them there with Anyala, my daughter, if you wish. We will return them to Kakut when the winter snows come."

The amusement faded from his voice.

"*Eeee.* We will take them back, as we took back the great canoe and placed it where it belongs . . . where it will always remain, so long as the people remain by the River and live in this land."

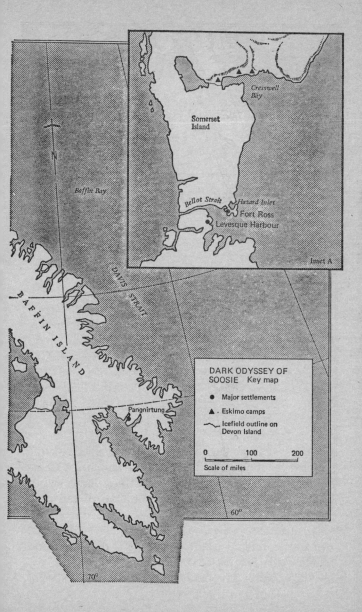

Somerset
Island

Cresswell
Bay

Baffin Bay

Bellot Strait   Hazard Inlet
Fort Ross
Levesque Harbour

Inset A

BAFFIN ISLAND

DAVIS STRAIT

Pangnirtung

DARK ODYSSEY OF
SOOSIE   Key map

● Major settlements

▲ Eskimo camps

— Icefield outline on
    Devon Island

0   100   200

Scale of miles

60°

70°

Dark Odyssey of Soosie

The federal day school at Spence Bay is an excrescence upon an alien face. Awkward and obtrusive, it clings to the perpetually frozen rock of the arctic coast some two hundred miles north of the Arctic Circle in a world belonging to another time.

On Friday night, April 15, 1966, the fluorescent lights of its largest classroom glared down upon a strange assembly. A gentle-faced and weary old man clad in the dark majesty of a judge's gown sat at the teacher's desk under a portable enamelled plaque which bore the colourful insignia of law and government. Facing him with an earnestness that was a grim parody on the daytime earnestness of the children whose places had been usurped, sixty or seventy men and women crowded into school desks, overflowed folding chairs, lined the walls, leaned on window sills or squatted on the floor.

Prominent in the foreground were several

R.C.M.P. officers in crimson ceremonial rig, four black-gowned lawyers, three or four immaculately dressed psychiatrists and physicians, several reporters and a clutch of employees of that burgeoning colonial empire, the federal Department of Northern Affairs. We were the intruders who had been flown to Spence Bay from as far afield as Newfoundland and Edmonton in order to ensure that justice was done, and was seen to be done, in this remote corner of the nation.

Massed solidly toward the rear of the room, unsmiling and unspeaking, were the others . . . the people whose land this was. They were colourfully clad in embroidered parkas, bright woollen sweaters and gaily coloured dresses, yet their mood was sombre. They did not look at the intruders in their midst. They did not even look at one another. They had been told to be here so they might witness what would be done with two young men of their own race who had transgressed against *our* law.

The Court of the Northwest Territories came to order.

> *Shooyuk E5-883 and Aiyaoot E5-22, both of Levesque Harbour, do jointly stand charged in that on or about the 15th day of July A.D. 1965, at or near Levesque Harbour, they did unlawfully commit capital murder of Soosie E5-20. . . .*

A reporter whispered a question to the government official sitting next to him: "What's going on? Do you give them prison numbers before you even try them?"

"Certainly not. Every Eskimo has a number like that. It makes them easier to identify."

Soosie E5-20 was dead. Shooyuk E5-883, who was her nephew, and Aiyaoot E5-22, who was the son of this woman none of us would ever know, stood before the judge as the court clerk read the charge against them. Their faces showed no comprehension even when the charge was translated by the court interpreter—a white man married to an Eskimo, who had lived among them for the best part of his life. It was clear to everyone present that the grave ritual in which the two accused were the central figures was incomprehensible to them. They stood before the judge, shrunken and withdrawn, two small, smooth-faced youths who did not seem much more than children; but they were men who had long since been driven from that world where children thrive.

The prosecution began its case at 9 A.M. the following morning, and by 11 P.M. sentence had been passed. During those hours we, the intruders, heard only the bare outline of how death came to one woman . . . fragments from the final chapter in a long, dark odyssey of a people's journey to destruction.

In the late summer of 1913 the Hudson's Bay Company established its most northerly post at Cape Dorset on the southwest coast of Baffin Island. The Eskimos there were a confident and effective people whose ability to hunt meat for their own use had sustained them through many generations; but before the decade ended they had become hunters of fur for the use of others and their lives had undergone a transformation. Instead of travelling in kayaks, they were making their way along the coasts in big gasoline-powered boats imported from Scotland; they were using expensive repeating rifles instead of bows and spears; and their families were eating flour bannocks, lard, canned ham and peaches instead of

174

country meat. Their summer tents, now made of canvas instead of skins, were filled with a plethora of trade goods ranging from gramophones to gaudy cotton clothes.

This is how things stood in the spring of 1926 when a daughter was born to a young man named Kitsualik. She was a fine big baby who, according to the old customs, should have been named after one of her ancestors. However, Christianity had been quick to follow the traders to Cape Dorset and the Church of England missionary christened the child Susannah. The people could not pronounce it, so they called her Soosie.

Soosie lived out her early childhood in the halcyon days of the fur trade. Trading posts were spreading like a fungoid growth across the arctic islands and along the mainland coast from Hudson Bay to the Bering Sea. It was a time when all but the most inaccessible Eskimos were being transformed from meat hunters into fox trappers, a time when the people were being weaned away from their old allegiance to the land and sea which had nurtured them since their beginnings.

Then suddenly, in 1930, with the advent of the Great Depression in the south, the cornucopia of the trading posts dried up. The price paid for a good white fox pelt plummeted from as much as a hundred dollars to five dollars or less, which in terms of what an Eskimo got for his money meant about fifty cents. Most of the smaller trading outfits packed up and abandoned the arctic, and famine followed upon their abrupt departure.

During 1931 and 1932 nearly three-quarters of the children born at Cape Dorset died of malnutrition and its attendant diseases in their first year of life. Soosie herself had watched her mother wrap the emaciated corpse of a baby brother in a piece of cloth and place it in a niche in the snowhouse wall so that the dogs could not get at it. The small body shared the snowhouse with the living until spring came and it was possible to bury him.

It was at this juncture that the Hudson's Bay Company, with an eye to the future after the Depression, made a proposal to the government. Canadian ownership of the immense, high arctic archipelago now known as the Queen Elizabeth Islands had been disputed by the United States, Denmark and other powers. The Company suggested that Canadian sovereignty over these vast, uninhabited lands be strengthened by settling them with Eskimos who had been "made indigent by the current economic problems." The Company volunteered to do the colonizing, and the government accepted with the proviso that the Company bear full responsibility for the well-being of the settlers and agree to repatriate them if they should ever become dissatisfied with their new homes.

In the autumn of 1933 the post managers at Cape Dorset, Pangnirtung on the west coast and Pond Inlet on the north coast of Baffin Island were told to begin recruiting colonists. It was no easy task, for the people were closely bound by tradition, familiarity and inclination to the places where their ancestors had lived and died. They had no wish to leave; and the Cape Dorset manager found no recruits until he sought the help of Kavavou, a sometime shaman who had become a "Company man."

Kavavou echoed the manager in extolling the virtues of a new country where game and fur abounded. He made much of the Company's promises of lavish new equipment to be provided free, together with an abundance of store food; and he confirmed the manager's assurance of passage home to any who might not be satisfied. A desperately hard winter, with hunger present in every igloo, gave such added weight to Kavavou's efforts that his cousin, Kitsualik, and a few other men reluctantly agreed to go.

When the Company's supply ship, *Nascopie*, steamed out of Cape Dorset harbour on August 14, 1934, she carried away with her six families—twenty-two men, women and children—together with their possessions and their dogs. One of those who stood at the rail watching the low hills of Cape Dorset grey into the distance was eight-year-old Soosie.

At Pangnirtung the settlers were joined by two families and at Pond Inlet by four more. Then the *Nascopie* steamed into Lancaster Sound and turned north toward the forbidding coast of Devon Island. On August 23 she dropped anchor at her destination, Dundas Harbour.

The colonists found themselves in a steep-walled fiord surrounded by an immense ice cap rising to six thousand feet, which left only a narrow fringe of ice-free rock along the base of the buried mountains. It was a land suitable for Titans but not for mortal men.

Although no Eskimo had ever chosen to live there, the place had been briefly occupied once before. In 1924 the federal government built an R.C.M.P. post at Dundas Harbour to command the entrance to Lancaster Sound as part of an early attempt to exert Canadian control over the high arctic islands. For a little while the Canadian flag whipped and frayed in the bitter winds funnelling off the ice cap, but the post soon had to be abandoned because the encroaching glaciers and the fearsome ice streams in the Sound so imprisoned the police that they could not patrol the land or travel out on the ice even to hunt seals with which to feed their dogs.

To the Cape Dorset settlers this forbidding place was utterly alien. They were used to a land of open tundra plain, not a mountainous world buried under perpetual ice. There were no caribou and few foxes or other animals on the meagre fringes of ice-free land. Because they were a people whose world was inhabited not only by the seen but by the unseen as well, the imponderable menace of this looming land shadowed them with apprehension.

Before two months had passed, the Cape Dorset people were longing to return to their own country. When the Company employee who was their guardian, and who lived in the comfortable police building, told them that nothing could be done until the ship returned the following summer, Kitsualik and three other men hitched up their dogs and set out to the west with their families, hoping to find the ice in that direction stable enough to let them escape across the Sound to northern Baffin Island.

It was a vain hope. After five days of tortuous travel on the shifting sea ice, during which they covered only forty miles, they were forced back to land at the mouth of Croker Bay. There they found westward travel along the shore barred by a succession of glacier tongues. Forced to retreat into Croker Bay (which was a slightly larger prison than Dundas Harbour), they spent the winter enduring worse privation than any they had known at Cape Dorset. They were able to survive only because Kitsualik revisited Dundas Harbour, abased himself before the angry white man and so obtained a dole of food.

Late in the summer of 1935 all the colonists gathered at Dundas Harbour determined to board the *Nascopie* and go home. But when the ship finally appeared, she anchored well offshore, unloaded some small quantity of supplies . . . and steamed away without them. They were told she would pick them up the following year.

The child, Soosie, remembered that second winter even more vividly than the first. While making a desperate attempt to hunt seals on the treacherous ice of the Sound during the dark days of January, Kitsualik was carried off when the shore-fast ice broke free of the land, sending him adrift in the running pack. Starving, and sheltering miserably behind upthrust slabs of ice on a piece of floe only a few yards across, he was driven eastward through nearly a week of below-zero weather before managing to scramble back to land. He had freed his dogs and abandoned his sled, so it took him the best part of another week to make his way back on foot to Croker Bay. By then his family had given him up for lost and hardly expected to be alive themselves to see the summer come.

The choice of Dundas Harbour for an Eskimo settlement might appear to have been a blunder, but this was not so. It was intentionally chosen to provide a justification for transporting Eskimos to new locations, on the grounds of strengthening national sovereignty, and so to establish an acceptable precedent for moving Eskimos to regions where they would be useful to the fur trade.

Separated only by the narrow gut of Bellot Strait, Boothia Peninsula and Somerset Island form a gigantic finger thrusting northward from the mainland of the central arctic. In the early 1930s this region still belonged to the Netchilingmiut—the Seal People—for no trader had succeeded in planting a permanent post among them. The Company had tried to do so from the westward as early as 1926 but had been rebuffed by shallow, ice-filled seas and by the Netchilingmiut themselves. They were a tough and touchy people whose preference for the old way of life was so strong that intruders bringing winds of change were made to feel unwelcome and even threatened.

In 1932 the Company had decided on a new assault on this last Eskimo redoubt, from the eastward through Lancaster Sound and Prince Regent Inlet, and at the same time had concluded that the best way to deal with the intransigence of the Seal People was to plant "domesticated" Eskimos in their midst. The Eskimos chosen for this role were the twelve Baffin Island families who had been set ashore at Dundas Harbour. In the autumn of 1935 the Company reported to the government authorities the surprising fact that Dundas Harbour had proved unsuitable and requested permission to move the people to a better site. Permission was quickly granted.

On a late August morning in 1936 the sonorous blast of the *Nascopie's* whistle again echoed from the cliffs surrounding Dundas Harbour. By the time she dropped anchor the entire population was ready to embark, and this time they were permitted to do so. One of Soosie's sisters recalled their feelings on that day.

"Everyone think now they going home. The bad times, they over now. Pretty soon we see all the people we leave behind. My father say he never go from Cape Dorset anymore."

When the *Nascopie* cleared the harbour she headed westward, bound not for Cape Dorset but for uninhabited Elizabeth Harbour on the south coast of Boothia. In her holds she carried prefabricated build-

180

ings and the supplies to establish a new trading post; but if the Baffin Island Eskimos aboard knew anything of this, they did not know they had been chosen to help make that post a successful venture.

A short distance into Prince Regent Inlet, the old ship encountered heavy ice . . . so heavy that after three days of bruising effort she was stopped. Her master decided to turn back, and two days later she anchored off the little Eskimo settlement of Arctic Bay at the northern tip of Baffin Island. A hurried decision had been made to offload the supplies for the new post, together with the settlers, and to pick them up the following summer for another attempt to reach the coast of Boothia.

The Pangnirtung men, who came of a stock wise to the ways of white men after nearly a century of contact with Baffin Bay whaling crews, seem to have suspected what was intended for them and obstinately refused to leave the ship. They would go home, they said, or they would go nowhere. The Pond Inlet people, whose home was only a hundred and fifty miles away and within reach by dog team, kept their own counsel.

Kitsualik and one or two other Cape Dorset men were for following the lead of the Pangnirtung people, but there was a strong detachment of R.C.M.P. travelling on the ship and Kavavou argued that the police would drive them ashore if they would not go voluntarily. Then a white man came among them to explain that it was too late for the *Nascopie* to return to Cape Dorset that season but, if the people were still of the same mind next summer, they would be taken home. So the Dorset group reluctantly disembarked along with the Pond Inlet families. The Pangnirtung people remained adamant; and when it became clear that force alone would move them, the Company officials reconsidered. A few days later these stubborn rebels were set ashore under the familiar mountains of their own land.

Again the Dorsets found themselves in alien country, this time surrounded by unfamiliar people speaking a different dialect. Hesitant to impinge on the hunting grounds of the Arctic Bay Eskimos, they huddled close to the settlement and, for the third successive year, they survived on the meagre dole issued by the Company. They were sustained by the enduring hope that they would be taken home when summer came again. The Pond Inlet people did not share that hope. As soon as travel conditions made it possible, they harnessed their dogs and slipped quietly away.

During that long winter the Company's plans suffered something of a sea change. Lorenzo Learmont, the post manager at Gjoa Haven on King William Island (which was as close to Boothia as the Company had been able to get from the westward), had long nursed a compulsive ambition to open the Netchilingmiut country to "the trade." During the winter of 1936 he persuaded his employers to try a dual assault. While the Company's small auxiliary schooner, *Aklavik*, attempted to reach Boothia from the west, the *Nascopie* would make a similar attempt from the east. If either ship succeeded, a post would be established at the mouth of Bellot Strait. If *both* made it, then the age-old dream of a commercially useful northwest passage would have been achieved. In either event, the Netchilingmiut would, to quote a Company historian, "be brought into the modern world."

Ice conditions during the summer of 1937 were exceptionally favourable. The little *Aklavik* managed to wiggle and worm her way through the pack to

Gjoa Haven, then on to Bellot Strait, and Lorenzo Learmont was on hand to greet the *Nascopie* when she arrived off the western entrance bearing the wherewithal with which to establish the new post of Fort Ross.

That wherewithal included the six Cape Dorset Eskimo families who had wintered at Arctic Bay and who, when they departed from that place aboard the *Nascopie*, still hoped they might be bound for home. But in the last days of August as they stood disconsolately on the rocky foreshore below the future site of Fort Ross and watched the smudge of the *Nascopie's* retreating smoke vanish into an autumnal sky, hope vanished with it.

Napachee-Kadlak remembered how his people felt that day.

"Now all know never go home again. Some women they cry and don't eat nothing. Nobody like this place. Netchilingmiut don't like to see strange people here. We don't know this country, don't know what to do."

The exiles could be of no value in advancing the Hudson's Bay Company's design as long as they remained in this hopeless state of mind. Somehow they had to be roused from their bewildered apathy. The solution was to send them a hundred and fifty miles to the north in a little motor boat, the *Seal*, to the uninhabited tip of Somerset Island where they would be forced by necessity to pick up the threads of life again while at the same time opening up a virgin source of furs.

The young man chosen to lead the little band of Dorsets and to manage the outpost, which was grandiloquently named Port Leopold, was Ernie Lyall, who had been a clerk in the Company's service for ten years. His was a happy choice as far as the Dorset people were concerned. Born on the Labrador coast, Lyall had Eskimo blood in his veins and sympathy and understanding for the people in his heart. He became a friend of Kitsualik's and eventually married Soosie's elder sister, Nipesha.

Lyall and his charges had a desperately hard time of it. Sea-ice conditions were nearly as bad as they had been at Dundas Harbour and the country roundabout Port Leopold was as inhospitable as the Netchilingmiut—who avoided all but a small part of the west coast of Somerset—had always known it to be. In 1940 the Company permitted the outpost to be closed.

Lyall brought the wanderers south; but with the exception of Kavavou and his family, they refused to go near Fort Ross. They wanted nothing to do with the white men there or with the Netchilingmiut whom they also distrusted and disliked. Instead, they chose to camp on the north shore of Creswell Bay which faces on Prince Regent Inlet some sixty miles north of Fort Ross. It was from here that they made a final plea to the Company, through Lyall, to be sent home to Cape Dorset. It was rejected. In fact, that same summer the *Nascopie* landed two additional Cape Dorset families who had been persuaded to join those who, so they had been told, were comfortably settled on Somerset Island.

When the *Nascopie* landed the newcomers, she disembarked another unseen and deadly passenger. Before October ended, fourteen of the Fort Ross immigrants were dead of influenza, including six of those who had camped at Creswell Bay.

As winter closed in, it brought famine with it. Fox pelts had become almost valueless and the men were unable to buy enough ammunition to make a sustaining hunt, let alone purchase sufficient quantities of food to meet the people's needs. Weak from the disease which had afflicted almost every man, woman and child, short of ammunition, and lashed by the violent blizzards which had made the east coast of Somerset infamous to the Netchilingmiut, the surviving Dorsets dubiously faced their first winter in this their sixth place of exile.

Although they were strangers to Creswell Bay, they suspected that the vicious northerly gales which had made Port Leopold untenable would strike as hard here, so they sought protection for their snowhouses close under a rampart of cliffs parallelling the north shore of the Bay half a mile inland. Kitsualik and his friend Tomasee chose to build their houses near the foot of the Bay where the cliffs dipped down and lost themselves in the inland plateau; but Jamesee, Johanee and a young man named Josee built theirs some miles to the westward where the cliffs rose nearly a hundred feet.

At fourteen years of age Soosie had now become a strikingly handsome woman who stood nearly a head taller than the rest of her people. She was sharply intelligent as well as a paragon of Eskimo domestic skills. Although she still lived with her family, she was betrothed to Josee. They had intended to marry in the autumn but because the epidemic had killed both Josee's father and his uncle, leaving him as the sole support of two widows and five children, his marriage to Soosie had to be postponed.

During December the gales roared down on Creswell Bay from across the polar sea with such fury that most of the time it was impossible to hunt seals at the breathing holes out on the wind-burnished ice. Meat became so scarce that dogs were dying and the people were growing gaunt with hunger.

During the winter the people spent at Arctic

Bay, Soosie's elder brother, Gideon, had begun to turn to the white men's religion seeking an eventual avenue of escape from the dismal existence of the exiles. This Christmas he held service in the chill darkness of the family snowhouse where seal oil had become too valuable to be burned in the lamps. It was a bleak and joyless parody of Christmas; nevertheless, Kitsualik's family was better off than Josee's, for that harassed young man had not managed to kill a seal for several weeks and the women and children in his igloo were surviving on the little that Jamesee and Johanee could spare.

During the first week in January the winds died down and it began to snow. Jamesee and Johanee moved their families into small travel igloos on the offshore ice in order to be near the sealing grounds. Josee considered doing likewise but, with eight people to house, he decided it would be best to leave the family where it was and do his sealing from Jamesee's igloo. Luck finally came his way and one afternoon he speared a big jar seal. He hauled it happily home to his snowhouse under the lee of the cliffs and that night he and the women and children feasted.

But the north wind began to blow again that night, and it blew a living gale. To Josee's family, well fed and warm for the first time in many days, the roar of wind reverberating through the walls of the snowhouse seemed no great threat and, as the hours slipped by, the sound grew muted and they went to sleep believing the storm was dying down. They did not know that the fury of the gale was being muffled by a torrent of snow driven over the edge of the cliff and building up in hard-packed layers above the snowhouse.

The next day when Josee crawled into the entrance tunnel he found it so solidly blocked that it took him an hour to cut his way out. When he finally broke through, it was to find the world enveloped in appalling turmoil.

"Snow was coming over the cliff like a river," he later described it. "Nothing could be seen. It was as if one's head was under freezing water. It filled up the hole I dug in the little time I had my head out. I could tell the igloo was already buried and I thought we better get out of there while we could."

Scrambling back into the interior of the igloo which, blanketed under the thickening drift and lit and warmed by seal-oil lamps, now seemed particularly snug, Josee urged the women to hurry and dress themselves and the children in their warmest outer garments. "We have to go!" he told them after describing the ferocity of the storm.

The women began to obey but then they paused. If the blizzard was so bad, how would they find shelter? Burdened by so many children, perhaps they would not be able to reach Jamesee's or Johanee's igloos even if they could find them in the blinding drift. No, they said at last, it would be better to stay where they were until the storm ended. If they could not dig their own way out, then Jamesee and Johanee would certainly come searching and would free them.

Nothing Josee could say would change their minds. He lingered in an agony of indecision for an hour or two before he made his choice. If they would not come with him, he would go alone.

The eldest child in that igloo was only ten but he considered himself a man and so was not prepared to obey the women. He struggled into his outer clothing and followed Josee into the tunnel. Several hours later man and boy crawled into Jamesee's igloo.

For another day and night the blizzard raged.

Then came a slight lull and Josee, Jamesee and Johanee fought their way to shore against a storm which was still strong enough to sometimes bring them to their knees. The ground drift was so thick they could see no marks to guide them in their search for Josee's igloo, and snow was rolling over the cliff like an avalanche. They persevered in their search until the wind began to rise again, forcing them to retreat to the shelter of the igloos out on the bay ice.

When the blizzard finally blew itself out and the short winter day broke clear and bright, the men hastened back toward the shore . . . to find themselves in a world so changed it was unrecognizable. An immense and faceless drift now sloped up from the beach to within a few feet of the crest of the cliff and stretched as far as the eye could see to east and west. All the familiar landmarks were obliterated and the three bewildered searchers had no way of determining where, under the mass of hard-packed snow, the igloo lay. Yet somewhere far beneath them two women and four children were entombed. Desperately they probed and dug, seeking some clue . . . but the snow revealed nothing of what it hid. They stood together and shouted at the top of their voices, and there was no answer from the depths. For nearly a week they sought to pierce that anonymous white shroud before, exhausted and borne down by sorrow, they accepted their defeat.

Early in February Josee drove a borrowed dog team into Fort Ross where he carefully described to the post manager how the tragedy had taken place. The manager radioed the nearest R.C.M.P. detachment, at Pond Inlet, and the police replied that a patrol—the first ever to be sent to Somerset—would soon be starting out and would investigate. Satisfied that he had done all that the white men required of him, Josee returned to Creswell Bay where in early April he and Soosie became man and wife.

On February 27 Constable J. W. Doyle, accompanied by two Eskimos, set out from Pond Inlet. Doyle travelled south across the mountains of Baffin Island to Foxe Basin, then turned east and north up the precipitous coast of the Brodeur Peninsula until he was abreast of Creswell Bay. On May 5 the three men had just completed the dangerous crossing of the broken ice of Prince Regent Inlet when they saw a dog team approaching. Its driver was Josee who had undertaken a hundred-mile journey from the starving Dorset camps in the hope of killing a polar bear.

Doyle accompanied Josee back to the camps where he found that "all the people were very hungry." He gave them what food he could spare but his own rations were running low so three days later, with Josee as his guide, he drove on to Fort Ross.

Josee's story had been under discussion there for several weeks and had become the subject of deepening suspicion. The white people believed Josee had at least been negligent and there were those who bluntly charged that he had abandoned his mother, aunt and four of the five children to free himself so he could marry Soosie.

"Eskimos don't have enough sense of responsibility," one of the white men who was present at Fort Ross remarked. "If things become too difficult, a man may just walk away and leave, and those remaining have to look after themselves. Even if Josee's story *was* more-or-less true, he should have stayed in the igloo with his family. It was despicable of him to run away."

With Lyall acting as interpreter, Josee was searchingly interrogated and in such a way as to make him understand what he was suspected of. Bewildered and deeply perturbed, he strove to placate his questioners by replying as he thought they wished him to reply, and in so doing succeeded only in reinforcing their belief that he was guilty.

It seems not to have occurred to his inquisitors that his visible distress could stem from the shame and horror of being thought capable of such crimes; but at least some of the white men must have known that to question an Eskimo even twice was to tell him that he was not believed . . . and an Eskimo accused of lying thinks of himself as an unworthy human being.

When, on May 18, Constable Doyle returned to Creswell Bay accompanied by Lyall, Kavavou, Takolik and the post manager, Josee went with them, not yet officially under arrest but, as his own people could see, an object of suspicion and distaste to the white men.

If there was to be a trial, Doyle needed the bodies of the missing people as evidence, so the five surviving men in the Dorset camp were dragooned into a work party together with Takolik, Kavavou and Josee, and set to digging for the buried igloo. For a few hours each day Josee was allowed to return to Kitsualik's camp . . . and to his young wife, Soosie. There are no records of what passed between them, but Josee became more and more withdrawn and silent as the days passed. Still, he did all he could to help the policeman and it was his persistence that finally led them to the place beneath which the igloo lay.

The searchers dug a shaft *thirty-four feet deep* before striking frozen ground. The snow was packed so hard it could only be cut with axes and it took eight men three days to sink the shaft. Then they drove a lateral tunnel in the direction Josee suggested and found the igloo.

It was empty, but Kitsualik soon found the place where the imprisoned people had tunnelled their way out. They had only been able to progress by filling in the tunnel behind them as they dug it out in front. The searchers tried to follow the same procedure but the work was so laborious and dangerous that Doyle decided to give it up and wait until summer suns melted the great drift.

He spent the next few months enjoyably as a guest of the Company at Fort Ross. Josee spent them at Creswell Bay in deepening darkness of the spirit. Except for Kitsualik and Soosie, people avoided him when they could. It was not that they believed him guilty of any crime, but he was under the shadow of a sword . . . the white man's sword of justice.

On August 4 Constable Doyle returned to Creswell Bay by boat. This time he found the bodies without which there could have been no legal case. The corpses told a ghastly story. Buried in utter darkness with little food or air, unable to judge or keep direction, they had burrowed blindly, not to the south where they might have found escape but westward along the foot of the cliffs under the deepest section of the drift. The women had led the way and at intervals behind them in the winding, twisting tunnel were the bodies of the children.

Josee was present when the bodies were removed from their snow crypts. That night when he did not return to Kitsualik's tent, Soosie went looking for him. She found him on the edge of the high cliff, a small, dark figure standing as immobile as the *inukok*—the stone semblances of men that some long-forgotten people had erected to give an effect of life to an otherwise empty land. Not life but death was in

Josee's face, but if he had it in mind then to make an end, Soosie's arrival forestalled him. Soosie was life . . . doubly was she so, for she was carrying his child.

Josee was taken back to Fort Ross by Doyle, this time under arrest. The *Nascopie* arrived on September 14 carrying the usual police detachment headed by a senior officer who was also a magistrate. Next morning Josee was arraigned before Inspector D. J. Martin and charged with criminal negligence resulting in the death of two women and four children. However, the *Nascopie's* master was anxious to depart so instead of being tried at once, Josee was remanded until the return of the *Nascopie* a full year hence.

Since there was no place to hold him at Fort Ross, he was released as a prisoner in his own custody and told to go back to Creswell Bay . . . and wait. Alone, he set out to walk seventy miles across the empty sweep of rock and tundra, oppressed by memories of the winter's tragedy, fearful of the incalculable vengeance of the white men, diminished and dishonoured in his own eyes and in the eyes of his people. It was more than could be borne. When he had approached to within only a mile of the skin tent wherein his young wife waited, Josee halted. He was near enough to see the beckoning glow of light through the translucent side of the tent, but the black pall that loomed behind him darkened his mind. Placing the muzzle of his rifle in his mouth, he leaned down and pulled the trigger.

Most of those at Creswell Bay accepted this new tragedy with resignation. Soosie alone dared to rage against those who had destroyed her husband. And when her child was stillborn that winter because another famine had weakened even her powerful body, her furious resentment against those who had brought her people to such a state of misery hardened into hatred.

Kitsualik tried to soothe her but she would pay no attention to him. The experiences of the past few years had aged him far beyond his forty-two years and he was no longer the man who had earned the respect of the Cape Dorset people. He no longer believed they could do anything for themselves except endure. If there was any leadership left it rested with Kavavou, but he had abandoned his fellow exiles to reëstablish himself as a creature of the Company, living close to the post and setting an example to the Netchilingmiut of how a man could expect to be rewarded if he changed from a seal hunter to a trapper of foxes.

That same year Kitsualik's son, Gideon, also abandoned his people to accompany a missionary to Arctic Bay and begin training as a priest of the white men's God. His departure filled Soosie with bitterness, and it took the last of the heart out of Kitsualik.

One savagely cold February night in 1942, when the people were enduring yet another epidemic, Kitsualik crawled out from under the robes where he had lain for several days in the grip of a raging fever. Dressing himself only in his sealskin trousers, he left the igloo so quietly that the others, sleeping fitfully, did not hear or see him go. Kitsualik had gone "walking on the land," having chosen to make an end to his long exile.

Soosie and her mother were left alone. But in the early spring of 1942 she married Napachee-Kadlak, Kavavou's youngest son, a gentle and ineffective man who was given to dreaming of other days and other places. He tried to persuade Soosie to abandon

Creswell Bay to go and live with his father's group at Levesque Harbour eight miles south of Fort Ross. Angrily she refused. Never again, she told him, would she place her trust in the *kablunait*. She saw only one hope for continuing survival, and it lay in the independent, self-sufficient way of life.

"She tell us," Napachee-Kadlak remembered, "we got to be *Innuit* again. We got to do like the old people used to do."

Napachee-Kadlak bent to her impassioned arguments, thereby hallowing the fact that the Cape Dorset exiles had found a leader in Kitsualik's daughter.

During the summer and autumn of 1942 Soosie goaded and guided her people through a frenzy of activity. Never before had they caught and dried so many fish. Never before had the men made such prolonged and successful journeys into the interior to hunt caribou. Never had they killed more white whales and bearded seals. By late September the Creswell Bay camp was adequately provisioned against the long night of winter for the first time since its occupancy.

To the south disaster loomed. Bad ice conditions had prevented the *Nascopie* from reaching Fort Ross with her cargo of supplies for the year ahead. Consequently, Kavavou's people at Levesque Harbour, who were almost totally dependent on the post, were soon in desperate need. When the R.C.M.P. sent a sled patrol to Fort Ross from Arctic Bay in March 1943 to bring in the mail the *Nascopie* had been unable to deliver, Constable DeLisle found fourteen destitute Eskimos at the post itself. He recorded that most of the Levesque Harbour people were sick, some with tuberculosis and many more because of another "flu epidemic" which had already killed several of them. One of the victims was Kavavou, whose reliance on the Company served him no better in the end than it had served Kitsualik.

Soosie's people had no contact with Fort Ross that winter and so were spared a new outbreak of disease. They hunted vigorously on the sea ice for seals and bears and, when their ammunition ran out, reverted to the use of spears. For the first time in many years the returning sun of spring was not obscured in mists of agony and sorrow.

During the summer of 1943 the Creswell Bay people continued to do well. Four children were born and one of them was Soosie's, a son whom she named Aiyaoot, in the old fashion.

It was a different matter at Levesque Harbour.

That summer the *Nascopie* again failed to reach Fort Ross and that remote little trading post suddenly became newsworthy. Headlines announced that two white men and the wife of one of them were marooned in the arctic with not enough food and fuel to last them through the winter. As soon as the autumnal ice was firm enough, Major Stanwell-Fletcher was parachuted down to direct the Eskimos in preparing an ice landing strip. When it was completed, a huge C-47 transport plane flew in and picked up the white people, taking them safely back to their own land. It did not carry away any of the Cape Dorset people who ten years earlier had been transported to Fort Ross from *their* own land.

Fortunately for the Levesque Harbour group, Ernie Lyall did not abandon them. Years later when he was asked why he had not taken the opportunity to escape in the plane, he found it hard to answer.

"Don't know why I stuck it out there. Things didn't look good at all, you know. Nothing left at the post and nothing to get from the country. Sure was hard to see that plane take off and head south, but my wife and kids, it was their people here, and I guess you'd say they'd sort of become my people too."

The white men had rescued their own, and the world applauded. It was left to Ernie Lyall to rescue the people the white men had abandoned, and the world knew nothing of it.

Accompanied by Takolik, who had succeeded his father Kavavou as nominal leader of the Levesque Harbour people, Lyall set out by dog team in the savage weather of early December to make his way to the nearest place from which help might be obtained. This was Arctic Bay, three hundred miles distant by the route the two men would have to follow—and which neither of them had travelled before. They took no food for their already starving dogs because there was none to take. They had no food for themselves either, except a little tea and three pounds of sugar. They had only about twenty rounds of ammunition—upon which their survival depended.

It took them a week to cross the treacherous expanse of broken pack in Prince Regent Inlet, but the ice was also their salvation for it brought them a polar bear. After landing on Baffin Island they became lost in the mountains, but they finally staggered into Arctic Bay. Although they made the return journey in better order, reaching Levesque Harbour in mid-January, their dog teams were able to haul so few supplies that these were exhausted by the end of February. Undaunted, Lyall set out to make another trip to Arctic Bay, returning in early April. Without his valiant help, most of the people at Levesque Harbour would undoubtedly have perished.

The people at Creswell Bay wintered well without any outside help. Jamesee and Napachee-Kadlak made a long trip into Prince Regent Inlet where they killed two bears and a huge square-flipper seal. Those who stayed at home were able to spear enough of the smaller jar seals to feed thirty-five human beings and to keep five dog teams in good condition. It no longer mattered very much to them that the Company had closed its trading post.

In early September 1944 an Eskimo from Levesque Harbour, who had gone to the Company's empty post to look for scrap metal for sled runners, hastened back wild with excitement. The ship had come! The *Nascopie* was anchored in the harbour! Within a few weeks the post was open again, but many of its customers had vanished.

Before his death in the winter of 1943, the most respected shaman of the Netchilingmiut had a vision in which he saw the whole of the northern region swept clean of mankind by some mysterious visitation. The old man warned his people to leave the north. They abandoned the upper portion of Boothia Peninsula and shifted far to the south and west.

If the Dorsets heard of the shaman's prophecy, they disregarded it. When the post reopened, the five families at Levesque Harbour returned to fox trapping with enthusiasm, for at the end of the war the price of white fox began to climb again. Soon the shelves of the trading post were loaded with such things as portable radios, sets of aluminum kitchenware, 20-horsepower outboard motors and gaudy articles of clothing made of new synthetic fibres. The Company had astutely concluded that Eskimos could best be encouraged to trap if they were offered a wide range of the elaborate and expensive consumer goods which were beginning to appear in southern stores.

Every effort was made to bring the Creswell Bay

people back into the fold, and the temptations offered by the glittering array of trade goods available at Fort Ross had their effect. Although Soosie fought fiercely to prevent it, individual families began to drift away to Levesque Harbour where they reverted to the trappers' way of life.

By the spring of 1947 only two families remained at Creswell Bay, and now Napachee-Kadlak insisted that he and Soosie and their children move south too. Dispirited by the weakness of her fellow exiles in allowing themselves to again be seduced into serving the white men and contemptuous of them because they would not see what she could see, Soosie reluctantly gave in.

"Very hard to make her go," Napachee-Kadlak remembered. "She say if we go only bad things happen."

Soosie was soon vindicated. In August the *Nascopie,* northbound on her annual supply run, struck a rock and sank . . . at Cape Dorset. Her loss, combined with the relatively small output of fur Fort Ross was producing, determined the Company to close that post for good. Early in 1948 the manager and his clerk, accompanied this time by Ernie Lyall, locked up the empty buildings and set off by dog sled to Gjoa Haven.

In the face of this final abandonment, Soosie tried vigorously to persuade her people to move back to Creswell Bay where they could still live off the land. At first she had little success because the people believed the Company either intended to build a new post south of Levesque Harbour or at long last repatriate them to Cape Dorset.

Soosie proclaimed these to be false promises, and such was her vehemence that even Takolik could not outface her. Her violent rejection of all that the white men stood for began to make people uneasy and when six families finally agreed to do as she demanded it was as much because of the desire to placate her as because they believed that she was right.

Shortly after the six families had reëstablished themselves at Creswell Bay and soon after the first gulls had returned to the land to proclaim the coming of spring, people began to sicken of an unknown and terrifying ailment. Some were asphyxiated when their muscles contracted around throats and chests. Some sank into comas from which, if they roused at all, they found themselves with crippled and useless limbs.

Unknown to himself or anyone else, it was a Netchilingmio come north to see if Fort Ross was really abandoned who had fulfilled the old shaman's prophecy by bringing the savage plague of poliomyelitis upon the Dorset people.

Soosie was several months pregnant when she was stricken, and again she lost her baby. Although the disease did not permanently cripple her in the flesh, it struck deep into her mind and spirit. During the rest of that year she was lost in a bottomless pit of black depression.

The outside world knew nothing of the new tragedy at Creswell Bay (and at Levesque Harbour where conditions were equally frightful) until mid-January of 1949 when Takolik was brought into Gjoa Haven by a party of Netchilingmiut who had found him wandering half-conscious on the ice of Rae Strait after his dogs died of starvation. Takolik had made his way across several hundred miles of unknown country to carry a message of distress, and it had taken him two months to make the journey.

In early February the R.C.A.F. dispatched a ski-equipped DC-3 to take a doctor of the Indian Health Service to the stricken camps. At Creswell Bay the doctor found several babies and eight older children and adults dead and the remainder so crippled or weakened from starvation that they could not hunt.

The DC-3 made several trips to ferry the worst cases out to hospital, shift the Creswell Bay survivors to Levesque Harbour (to which place Ernie Lyall had temporarily returned), and to bring in food and clothing. It was the first assistance proffered to the Baffin Island people during all the long years of their exile.

Early in that fatal winter of 1948–1949 an ironic coincidence had brought Lorenzo Learmont back to Fort Ross, for whose establishment he, more than any other, had been responsible. He came in a new guise —as an archaeologist employed by a museum to dig into the past history of the Eskimos . . . but found himself observing the actual dissolution of a people. It was he who sent the message describing the Cape Dorsets' plight which Takolik carried to Gjoa Haven. One wonders what his thoughts were as he looked upon the wreckage of the dream that he had fathered.

Early in the summer of 1949, Lyall and his family moved south to Spence Bay where the Company had just established a new post serviced from Tuktoyaktuk in the western arctic. Spence Bay was on the west side of Boothia in the middle of the Netchilingmiut country and distant six or more days hard driving by dog team from Fort Ross. During the months between spring thaw and autumn freeze-up, it was virtually inaccessible to the Cape Dorset people, who had remained at Levesque Harbour not because it was a good place but because they were so distressed in mind and body, so unmanned by apprehensions, that they were unable to muster the will to leave. They could not face another dislocation to a new place of exile such as Spence Bay represented; nor could they go home to Cape Dorset. Permission to do so was refused by the authorities who thereafter turned their backs on the Levesque Harbour people, effectively ignoring their existence through the whole of the ensuing decade.

Although the bottom dropped out of the white fox trade again in 1949 so that the people could obtain very little from the post at Spence Bay even when they could make the long journey, they clung to life and even made some progress toward their own regeneration.

In 1953 a scientific expedition happened their way and one of its members spent a few hours with Napachee-Kadlak and Soosie.

"She was a formidable woman. Good looking, the biggest Eskimo I ever saw. Getting stout but active and energetic. She had three or four kids and kept them in great form even though the whole bunch was in tough shape when we arrived. They were out of ammunition and had had poor luck in the spring sealing. Soosie made me nervous though. She had a way of looking past you, as if she could see things you didn't know were there."

The following year Takolik and two other families moved to Spence Bay to live on the welfare and family allowance benefits which more and more Canadian Eskimos were coming to rely upon.

Soosie, who had regained some of her lost influence, fiercely opposed the idea of moving. During the tragic events of 1948–1949 her behaviour had sometimes been so erratic as to frighten those around her but these moods had gradually become less frequent and she seemed to be returning to her own indomitable self . . . until the spring of 1958 when an epidemic of what may have been measles killed three children, one of whom was hers.

"She go crazy then," Napachee-Kadlak remembered. "She say white man trying to kill all babies so there going to be no more Innuit. When someone say now maybe we should go to Spence Bay, she say she going to kill herself and me and the children before she do that."

It was then that authority intervened for the second time in the lives of the people at Levesque Harbour. One summer day an Otter float plane arrived carrying an R.C.M.P. constable and an official of the Department of Northern Affairs. The people were gathered together and told that all children of school age were to be taken away; that they must go to a boarding school somewhere in the south and would not be returned to their parents until the summer of the following year.

"This was worse thing for us," recalled Napachee-Kadlak. "Worse thing than hunger or T.B. We love our children. Now we not have them anymore."

A month after the children were removed, the Otter returned and flew the Levesque Harbour people, eight at a time, to Spence Bay where they underwent their first examination for tuberculosis. Those most badly afflicted were shipped south for treatment. Some did not return for years . . . others died in ultimate exile.

Midway into her seventh pregnancy, Soosie had reacted to the removal of her older children by suffering a complete breakdown. The doctor who saw her at Spence Bay ordered her evacuated to a mental hospital in Alberta . . . and it is at this point that we pass through the door at the end of the long, dark corridor that is the fateful past of Soosie and her people, to emerge abruptly into the harsh glare of the classroom at Spence Bay. It is here, at the beginning of the end, that we who were the intruders in that land first looked upon that which we had wrought.

In the crowded room an eminent psychiatrist testified before the silent people:

". . . her symptoms were those of an anxiety neurosis . . . she was exceedingly disturbed . . . recovery was slow, but after the birth of her child she seemed to make some progress. . . ."

Soosie was returned to Levesque Harbour after several months in hospital, but in 1964 she again retreated from her broken world . . . this time in a strait jacket. Six months later, after enduring shock treatments, she was pronounced cured and sent home again . . . home to a pocket of humanity that had shrunk to three women, five men and eleven children. What had been done to Soosie could not be cured so easily.

On July 6, 1965, she vanished out of time, and in her place appeared a visitation spawned by the winds of madness.

The woman who had struggled so fiercely to preserve her people now threatened to become their nemesis. Raging through the camp, tearing her hair out in handfuls, screaming threats at those she met, she brought a new dimension of terror to a people who were at the end of their tether. Picking up her baby daughter, she flung the child to the ground. She pursued other children, pelting them with rocks. She struck against the very stuff of life by destroying the hunting and fishing gear. Sanity was tottering at Levesque Harbour. Reality was drifting away....

In the school room we listened to the testimony of Kadluk, father of Shooyuk.

"She tell everybody now she have to kill them. She go around trying to blow her breath on everybody to make them crazy too. We had to keep her off. We couldn't help it because she was after the people. Three men caught her and she fought them very hard but they tied her up. But she always got loose. Three times she got loose...."

There was one brief and pitiful respite. Desperately trying to calm his wife, Napachee-Kadlak played Soosie a tape sent to them by some of their relatives at Cape Dorset.

"It brought back memories of the times we are children in Cape Dorset and we are real happy. Soosie was good then, not mad at all. She was real happy then...."

It was a final, dying gleam.

A few hours later she was again running through the camp, screaming that God had told her to kill everyone so that all would at last be free. But the two women, five men and eleven children fought with desperation to retain their hold on life.

They could neither escape nor send for help because the sea ice was breaking up, and it was impossible to travel over it or across the swollen rivers on the sodden land. But they dared not stay near Soosie who even in ordinary times was a match for any of them and who now was armed with a madwoman's fearsome strength.

Kadluk told us of their hard dilemma:

"One morning she jump on Napachee-Kadlak

204

and try to kill him and we just get her away, then she go to the dogs and kill some dogs. Then we know we got to go somewhere."

On July 12 they fled across the shifting ice to a barren islet lying half a mile offshore. They could take only what little gear they could carry on their backs. On that bleak reef, beleaguered by dread, they waited, hoping for a miraculous deliverance—praying, in their extremity, to *our* God for help.

Hour by hour through the circle of almost perpetual daylight they watched the shore through Kadluk's old brass telescope.

"We very scared she take a knife and come out to kill the people. We very hungry because too scared if we go away hunting she might come to the women and children. Now we see her throwing our things into the water. She is looking as if she is watching things where there is nothing. She takes everything and shakes it, shaking the devil out of it. She has all the tents torn down and smashing the poles. We are watching her breaking up our gear. She want to kill us because she want us to be saved. The devil is telling her what to do. . . ."

For three sleepless days and nights they waited and watched, then could wait no longer. The women and children were in terror. There was no food, and unless she was stopped, Soosie would destroy everything in the camp.

On the morning of July 15 Napachee-Kadlak and Kadluk spoke to Shooyuk and to Soosie's son, Aiyaoot. They were young and strong, and there was a task ahead that would require strength.

"I tell them they have to go back. She have to stop smashing everything. Someone have to stop her. I tell them to get the knives away from there but if

205

she don't come after you, don't do anything to her. I love my wife and don't want her to be hurt. But if she come after them, they better shoot. . . ."

Fearfully the two young men approached the shore. When Soosie saw them she came running, screaming imprecations. They fired to one side, hoping to frighten her away, hoping even then to stave off the inevitable. But still she ran toward them, swaying and swerving and waving her arms. The rifles crashed again. Soosie E5-20, who had spent twenty-nine of her thirty-nine years as an exile, had been given her release.

Those who remained were not so fortunate.

In late August when the police plane came to take the children away to school, Napachee-Kadlak handed the constable a sheaf of wrapping paper covered with the syllabic script which he had been taught by the missionary at Cape Dorset so many years before. It was a complete and detailed account of everything that had taken place at Levesque Harbour between July 5 and July 15.

The subsequent R.C.M.P. investigation took a long time to complete. Meanwhile, the people at Levesque Harbour, believing that their explanation of why they had to kill Soosie had been accepted, were trying to put the hideous days of July behind them and repair what little was left of the tattered fabric of their lives.

In October Aiyaoot and Shooyuk were sent to Spence Bay to buy ammunition for their winter hunt. Immediately upon arrival Shooyuk was arrested, charged with capital murder and flown off to jail in Yellowknife eight hundred miles to the southwest.

In Yellowknife, the Crown Attorney, David Searle, studied the police reports and concluded that the charge should be dropped or at least reduced to one of justifiable manslaughter. He could see no useful purpose in adding new agonies to those the people at Levesque Harbour had already endured and he so advised the Department of Justice in Ottawa.

He was ordered to proceed with the case as originally charged.

The guardians of justice who act on our behalf chose to press the charge of wilful murder not just against Shooyuk (and Aiyaoot who was co-charged with murder sixty minutes before the trial began) but in effect against all the survivors of the tragedy, since the young men had acted on behalf of them all. They chose to sentence this handful of tormented people to a new ordeal of fear and black uncertainty through a *full seven months* until a "proper show trial" could be staged.

The men who made this choice remain cloaked in anonymity. They were senior officials of the Departments of Justice and of Northern Affairs; and this decision was part of a greater one, for our government had concluded that the time had come for all Eskimos (and Indians) to conform fully to our concept of law and our version of morality. The time had come when men, women and children, such as those forlorn remnants of the dispossessed who lingered on at Levesque Harbour, should each be made to pay for the essential crime of failing to be born as one of us.

It was a decision which made victims of Eskimos and white men alike. There was not one among the intruders—who had been brought at such expense to Spence Bay to give force to the farce of justice—who was not wracked with agony on behalf of the accused . . . and with guilt on behalf of our just society.

In a voice taut with suppressed emotion, the Crown Attorney twice apologized to the jurors for doing what he had to do. He was no more torn within himself than was one worldly reporter from Toronto who, in the early dawn of the day following the trial, stood on a headland overlooking the settlement and wept. An R.C.M.P. constable who was marooned for eight bitter February days at Levesque Harbour while investigating the case, and who was fed and sheltered by the very people he was to bring to justice, was as much a victim as was Ernie Lyall, the court interpreter, who, knowing and loving the people, found himself the instrument through which they, in their innocence, convicted themselves of having trespassed against our law.

All these and more were victims; but perhaps chief among the victims of our race was Judge John Sissons. As judge of the Northwest Territorial Court for fifteen years, he had fought a stubborn battle with the legal bureaucrats in Ottawa to temper our justice to the realities and ancient usages of Eskimos and Indians. At Spence Bay what John Sissons had tried to accomplish was as much on trial as were the two defendants. And in his way he was as helpless as they, for he too was pinioned within the legal cage.

The members of the jury were also victims of the worm of guilt—and that was fortunate, for it was they who denied the policy makers in Ottawa the total victory they sought. The jury acquitted Aiyaoot, and although finding Shooyuk guilty of manslaughter, recommended mercy. Then at last Judge Sissons was freed from his cage. In a shaking voice he committed Shooyuk to two years suspended sentence, telling him to go home to his own people and "try to forget the things that have happened to you and try to live a good and happy life."

He should not himself be judged for the terrible

irony of those words. They were said with hope and pity, but it was too late for that.

By trial's end Napachee-Kadlak, husband of Soosie and father of Aiyaoot, had become a shambling, incoherent travesty of a man whose mind dwelt only in the past. Shortly after the trial, Kadluk, father of Shooyuk and one of the chief witnesses for the prosecution, tried to drown himself in the swirling waters of Bellot Strait not far from the ruins of Fort Ross. One had only to look into the faces of Aiyaoot and Shooyuk to know that these young men, who had been the last strength of a broken people, were now themselves forever broken. Some of the people would survive in the flesh a little while longer, but the spirit within them was dead.

I spoke to Kadluk a few hours before the aircraft carried us back to our own world. I spoke to him not for his sake but for my own. Groping for words, I tried to tell him of the shame that burned in some of us because of what had been done to him and to his people.

His gaze was fixed on a patch of black rock emerging from the snows at his feet. After a while he murmured, "*Ayorama* . . . there is no help for it."

ABOUT THE AUTHOR

For over thirty years FARLEY MOWAT has written of the lands, seas and peoples of the Far North with a humor and a raciness, and understanding and compassion that place him internationally among Canada's most distinguished authors.

Born in Belleville, Ontario, in 1921, Mowat grew up in Belleville, Trenton, Windsor, Saskatoon, Toronto and Richmond Hill as his librarian father moved a household that included a miniature menagerie around the country; those early adventures were chronicled in *Owls in the Family* and *The Dog Who Wouldn't Be*. During World War II Mowat served in the army, entering as a private and emerging with the rank of captain. The experience of battle seared the imagination of the young soldier and ultimately gave rise to his most recent book, *And No Birds Sang*, a gripping eyewitness account of combat in Italy and Sicily.

Following his discharge, Mowat renewed his interest in the Canadian Arctic, an area he had first visited as a young man with an ornithologist uncle. Since 1949 he has lived in or visited almost every part of Canada and many other lands, including the distant regions of Siberia. He has said of himself, "I am a Northern Man . . . I like to think I am a reincarnation of the Norse saga men and, like them, my chief concern is with the tales of men, and other animals, living under conditions of natural adversity." His experiences have inspired such works as *People of the Deer, The Desperate People, Never Cry Wolf, A Whale for the Killing, The Boat Who Wouldn't Float, Lost in the Barrens* and *Grey Seas Under*. Farley Mowat's twenty-five books have been published in over twenty languages in more than forty countries.